ART AND HISTORY
OF
FLORENCE

MUSEUMS · GALLERIES · CHURCHES · PALACES · MONUMENTS

335 COLOR PICTURES
INCLUDING RESTORED WORKS OF ART

BONECHI

* * *

© Copyright by Casa Editrice Bonechi, via Cairoli 18/b - 50131 Firenze - Italia
Tel. 055/576841 -   - Fax 055/5000766

Printed in Italy by Centro Stampa Editoriale Bonechi.

ISBN 88-7009-422-7

English translation: Erika Pauli *for* Studio Comunicare, Florence.

This publication has been prepared by the editorial staff of the Publishing House.
The text of the History of Florence was taken from the Enciclopedia della Toscana
paese per paese *and was adapted by Renato Stopani.*

The photographs are the property of the Archives of the Publishing House Bonechi and were taken by:
Gaetano Barone, Carlo Cantini, Paolo Giambone, Stefano Giusti, Italfotogieffe, Antonio Lelli,
Andrea Pistolesi, Antonio Quattrone, Alessandro Saragosa, Soprintendenza Archeologica
per la Toscana, Soprintendenza ai Monumenti di Firenze.

All our tourist editions are periodically updated. The photographs in this recently produced book were made specifically for this publication. The works of art reproduced are therefore shown as they are to date. He wish, however, to specify that the Gates of Paradise on pages 59 and 60 have recently been replaced by a copy. In this case we chose to leave the photo of the original. The doors are at present being restored and the finished panels can be seen in their original splendor at the Museo dell'Opera del Duomo, where Ghiberti's masterpiece will be housed in its entirety to safeguard it from the damages produced by time and atmospheric agents.

Other monuments, palaces and churches are also currently being restored: in these cases we have used archive photos while waiting for the completion of the work.

BRIEF HISTORICAL SURVEY

	8th - 1st cent. B.C.	1st - 10th cent.	11th - 12th cent.	13th cent.
HISTORICAL SOCIAL AND ECONOMIC EVENTS	- Already occupied in prehistoric times, an Etruscan settlement is formed as early as the 8th cent. B.C. to control the ford across the Arno where the Ponte Vecchio now stands. In 59 B.C. the Roman colony of *Florentia* is founded. 	- The spread of Christianity begins in the 4th cent. and the first churches are built. With the fall of the Empire come the invasions of the Ostrogoths (405), Byzantines (539), Goths (541), and Lombards (570). In the Carolingian period (8th cent.), a feudal system is installed and Florence becomes a county of the Holy Roman Empire.	- Florence, by now a commune, clashes with neighboring communes such as Fiesole, which is besieged and partially destroyed. 	- The Commune of Florence becomes more important, despite the struggles between Guelphs (supporters of the pope) and Ghibellines (supporters of the Germanic Emperors). The emergence of the « *popolo grasso* » (wealthy middle class) backed by the Guelphs leads to a policy of open struggles for supremacy with the neighboring Tuscan communes. The aristocratic classes see their power diminish as economic development leads to the rise of the classes of entrepreneurs, merchants, and bankers, who form the Arti Maggiori (Major Guilds). From the middle of the century on communal power is in their hands. There is a notable increase in population.
TOWN PLANNING	- The Forum, the *Capitolium*, a theater, an amphitheater and walls are to be found around the two main streets of the Roman colony (Via Roma - Via Calimala and Via Strozzi - Via del Corso). The town, even though small and self-contained, serves as an intermediate stopping point which controls the important trade routes between North and South and the coast and the hinterland that had already existed in Etruscan times.	- While many buildings had gone up in the Roman period (now buried and identified in recent archaeological excavations), with the fall of the Empire (and even before, with the Byzantines), the city, a trading center, shrinks. It makes a comeback to more active economic life in the Carolingian period. Once the first churches have been built (S. Lorenzo), the circuit of city walls is enlarged and suburbs spring up outside the main city gates.	- The circuit of walls is extented to include the left bank of the river and the Baptistery and San Miniato al Monte are built. The affirmation of the communal life leads to a more active economy and a resulting increase in population. 	- The city consists of tower-houses, easy to defend in case of attacks by other Florentine factions. The network of city streets becomes particularly complicated. Palazzo Vecchio and the Duomo are built in the new Gothic style, together with the Bargello.
ART AND CULTURE	- No outstanding artistic remains of Etruscan civilization have survived in the urban area of Florence: in the neighboring towns mention can be made of the tombs of Sesto Fiorentino, the temple and the walls of Fiesole, the funerary stelae near Pontassieve. The cultural aspects of the area fall into a cultural pattern that is typical of Etruscan northern Tuscany.	- The cultural and artistic life of the Roman city dies as a result of the invasions and continues only in the field of religion. From the 8th cent. on, culture receives new stimulus from the Carolingian schools.	- Romanesque art affirms itself. In Florence it is characterized by an external facing of polychrome marble. Sculpture becomes a self-sufficient work of art as well as an element of architecture. Painting, however, continues to depend on the Byzantine tradition. 	- The Gothic style, which originated in France, spreads. But it loses some of the airiness and thrust skywards which characterize the style; examples in Florence are Santa Maria Novella and Santa Croce. Painting in Florence is highlighted by the emergence of two great figures, Cimabue and Giotto. Even though the former is still bound to proceding schemes, he is aware of the problems of mass and relief, as can be seen in his Crucifix in Santa Croce and the Maestà in the Uffizi. Giotto transmits a feeling of real three-dimensionality with his work, a realism of expression and of setting.

14th cent.	15th cent.	16th - 17th cent.	18th - 19th - 20th cent.
- When the kings of Naples and England default in prepaying large debts, the domination of the middle classes is threatened by the resulting crises. After the tyranny of the Duke of Athens in the middle of the century and the plague of 1348, there are various revolts by the lower classes. The middle classes, whose power has been consolidated, begin to oppress the lower classes, who rebel with Ciuto Brandini and then with the Ciompi Revolt, where they succeed in driving out the Priors and forming three new Guilds, which participate briefly in the government of the city.	- The wealthy classes once more gain in importance; the principal Florentine families (Pitti, Capponi, Alberti, Uzzano, Albizi, Medici) struggle for supremacy, In 1433 the Medicis prevail with Cosimo the Elder: his grandson Lorenzo was to become the key figure in the European politics and culture of the period. Later, Piero de' Medici would surrender to Charles VIII. The city continues to flourish economically throughout the century while in the latter part of the 15th century the popular need for democracy and a religious reform come to a head in the figure of Girolamo Savonarola.	- The return to power of the Medici is consolidated by the election of Giovanni de' Medici to pope. The presence in Italy of Charles V of Spain leads to a revolt, followed however by the return to the throne of Alessandro de' Medici. Cosimo creates the regional state. Little by little life in the city loses its initial impulse; Florence stops expanding and the grand duchy, the commercial power, becomes primarily agricultural.	- In the 18th cent. the Hapsburg-Lorraine dynasty is at the head of the Grand Duchy, and thanks to various reforms, the economy takes on new life with Pietro Leopoldo. After the French domination between the 18th and 19th cent., the Lorrainers reclaim the Chiana and the Maremma. Despite overtures to the liberals, a triumvirate to the concession of the Constitution is constituted. The abolition of the corporations which still date back to the Middle Ages, and the relaunching of small farm holdings by the Lorrainers, are followed up by pressure from the liberals who, having obtained the statute, the freedom of the press and the presence of the civil guard (1847), now intend to obtain the constitution from the Grand Duke, up to the point where he is expelled. The grand duke Leopold II, after fleeing from the city, returns with the protection of the Austrians, but is forced to leave for once and all in 1859. Annexed to Piedmont, in 1855 Florence is the capital of Italy.
- The Ponte Vecchio, part of the Duomo, Giotto's Campanile, Palazzo Vecchio, Orsanmichele and the Loggia of Bigallo date to this period. In the first half of the century new order is conferred on the city by the construction of the third, and largest, city wall, which also embraces vast areas Oltrarno. Here the remains can still be seen, while on the right bank only the city gates have survived the 19th-century rebuilding.	- Numerous palaces are built for the wealthiest Florentine families (Pitti, Medici) and other monuments Inspired by the geometric laws of antiquity. Brunelleschi, with superb simplicity, designs Santo Spirito, San Lorenzo, the Pazzi Chapel, and the Dome for the Duomo.	- The changes that the city undergoes in the 16th century are a result of the grand-ducal cultural policy, and after the construction of the Laurentian Library of the New Sacristy by Michelangelo, the city is enriched by the Uffizi, the Logge del Pesce, Boboli Gardens, the Logge of the Mercato Nuovo and the Bridge of Santa Trinita, as well as numerous private palaces. Mannerist structures with tendencies at times for the peculiar appear between the 16th and the 17th century. On the whole, however, urban building activity slows up in the 17th cent. and is generally limited to a retouching or renovation of extant works.	- As regards town planning, in the 18th cent. unhealthy dwellings for the poor take over the center, while the middle classes built up their own distinctive residential districts. The installation of the two railroad stations is followed by a restructuration of the center and the demolition of the walls to reclaim the slums and make the city more prestigious (projects by Poggi). As the capital, the rapidity of the industrial and demographic development of the city leads to damage which has still not been repaired (subdivision of green areas and living spaces, traffic, economic choices). In the 20th cent. the new railroad station of S. Maria Novella is built (G. Michelucci), followed by the destruction in the war of the bridges over the Arno (only the Ponte Vecchio was to escape destruction).
- In sculpture great artists are at work: Arnolfo di Cambio, who designed the facade of the Duomo that is no longer extant, as well as outsiders such as Tino di Camaino, Andrea and Nino Pisano. The figure of Giotto influences the entire peninsula and in the city generates a school which includes Taddeo Gaddi, Maso di Banco, Bernardo Daddi. In the middle of the century, Andrea Orcagna and Nardo di Cione come to the fore, together with many other artists whose works still today enrich the city's churches. In the field of literature there is Dante, Boccaccio and Petrarch. The « stil novo » and the Divine Comedy make the vernacular a language to be reckoned with on an international level, marked by the Florentine characteristics .	- The concept of the rationalization of art develops in the cultural circles of this period, which is called Renaissance. Inspiration draws from classic art and a scrupolous analysis of perspective and the concept of space open the doors to the works of Donatello, Masaccio, Botticelli, Ghiberti, Fra Angelico, Michelozzo, Alberti, Della Robbia, Paolo Uccello, Pollaiolo, Lippi and Brunelleschi.	- Early Renaissance forms limit the 16th cent. artists too closely, for what they now want to express is man's new desire to dominate nature, as in the works of Leonardo da Vinci, Michelangelo, Raphael, Andrea del Sarto, until the news conditions of life will focus in the sensibilities of Mannerism. From there, through the works of the Carracci and Caravaggio, the next step is the Baroque. Artists of this period are Cellini, Vasari, Giambologna, and in literature, Machiavelli, while the Accademia della Crusca and del Cimento see the light of day.	- In the 19th cent. the dictates of the Accademia di Belle Arti, bound to the political dictates, influence the sculpture of Dupré and Bartolini. The works of Cecioni, indebted to the fresh spontaneity of the Macchiaioli painters, is quite something else. dedicated to a rupte with the academicism of the Ussi and the Benvenuti, the Macchiaioli also use spots of color to depict subjects of dayli life that are generally disgregator. Besides Fattori, mention must Besides Fattori, mention must be made of Signorini, Costa, Lega. In the 20th cent. Rosai and Corti work in Florence. In the broader fiel of culture, the presence of the nucleus of the Futurists must be noted. Art in the city however is seriously damages by the flood of November 4, 1966, which destroys or harms any number of works.

FROM THE BEGINNINGS TO THE THIRTEENTH CENTURY

The recent archaeological excavations in Piazza della Signoria have furnished evidence that present day Florence was already occupied in prehistoric times. Other signs document the presence of a village in the early iron age and in Etruscan times. But the real foundation of the city dates to Roman times and the oldest part of the city with its network of streets in an orthogonal pattern bears the imprint of these Roman origins. What the earliest chronicles had to say about the origins of the city, albeit in fable form, seems therefore to be based on fact. When it originated as one of Caesar's colonies, the operations involved in founding the *castrum* and the division of the land into *centuriae* began in the spring of 59 B.C., at the time of the *ludi florales* (the probable source of the name *Florentia*). The colony was laid down following the axis of the consular Via Cassia, which ran along the northern edge of the Florentine basin. For the sake of defense, the city was set at the confluence of two streams (the Arno and the Mugnone) where the oldest populations had previously been located.

Rectangular in plan, it was enclosed in a wall about 1800 meters long. The built-up area, like all the cities founded by the Romans, was characterized by straight roads which crossed at right angles. The two main roads led to four towered gates. The *decumanus maximus* (at present the streets of the Corso, Speziali and Strozzi) and the *cardo maximus* (Piazza San Giovanni, Via Roma and Via Calimala) converged on a central square, the *forum urbis* (now Piazza della Repubblica) where the Curia and the Temple dedicated to the Capitoline Triad (Jupiter, Juno, and Minerva) were later to rise. The topography of the city differed in its orientation from that established by the division of the surrounding land into *centuriae*, whose axis was, as mentioned, the Via Cassia. The *castrum*, on the other hand, adhered to the classical ritual of an orientation based on the cardinal points.

Archaeological finds, many of which came to light during the course of works which «gave new life» to the old city center, have made it possible to locate and identify the remains of various important public works: the Capitoline Baths, the Baths of Capaccio, so-called from the point of arrival of the aqueduct from Monte Morello: «Caput aquae» (head of the waters = Capaccio), the sewage system, the pavement of the streets, the Temple of Isis (in the Piazza San Firenze) and other lesser temples, the Theater (now the area is occupied by the back of the Palazzo Vecchio and by the Palazzo Gondo) and the Amphitheater, whose perimeter is still to be seen in the curve of various streets: Via Torta, Via Bentaccordi, Piazza Peruzzi. Some of these buildings were outside the walls (the Theater and the Amphitheater, for example) which testifies to the urban development of the original settlement, probably as early as the 1st century B.C. The Arno was also outside the walls (the city developed on the right banks), with a river port that constituted an important infrastructure for the city, for in Roman times the river was navigable from its mouth up to its confluence with the Affrico, upstream from Florence.

The location of the city at a spot where it was relatively easy to cross the Arno had not been left to chance and was typical of the centers that originated as potential bridgeheads. In fact a bridge was built here probably around the 1st century B.C., the first bridge in Florentine history, in all likelihood somewhat upstream from today's *Ponte Vecchio*. In the overall picture of the Roman territorial organization *Florentia* was the focal point of a district in which its function as a city balanced its status of thoroughfare, with the bridge over the Arno keeping the communication routes in the hills to the south in touch with those of the Appenine crossings.

The city developed rapidly thanks to its favorable position and the role it played in the ambit of the territorial organization in the region. It soon superceded Arezzo as the leading center in northern Etruria and was chosen as the seat of one of the *correctores Italiae*. Economic power was the driving force behind the urban growth of the young colony. Commercial activity and trade thrived thanks to the fact that important communications routes (land and water) intersected at *Florentia* and offer an explanation for the presence of those oriental merchants, probably on their way from Pisa, who first introduced the cult of Isis and then (2nd century) Christianity.

The earliest indications of the Christian religion are bound to the cults of the deacon Lorenzo and the Palestinian saint, Felicita. Both first arose in the suburbs, the districts which had risen outside the walls along the consular roads which left the city. It was there that the oldest Florentine churches were built: *San Lorenzo* consecrated in 393, the first diocese, and *Santa Felicita*, whose origins go back to the 4th-5th centuries. According to legend, Saint Miniato, one of the members of the first Christian community, also came from the east. Together with eight of his companions he was martyred in the year 250 during the persecutions ordered by Decius. The Florentines do not however seem to have had a bishop prior to the late 3rd century. The first one recorded is San Felice who participated in a Roman synod in 313. It is interesting to note that contacts with the East continued. The most famous of the early Florentine bishops, San Zenobius, who lived in the early 5th century, also had an oriental name and, as early as the 7th century, Reparata, another Palestinian saint, was worshipped.

THE BYZANTINE, LOMBARD AND CAROLINGIAN PERIODS

The Barbarian invasions seriously impaired the importance of *Florentia*. In 405, even though gravely damaged, the city managed to halt the hordes of Radagaisus, which were defeated by Stilicho but later it could not avoid being involved in the disastrous Gotho-Byzantine war. Its strategic position as bridgehead on the Arno and strong point in the communications route between Rome and Padania explains why the city was so keenly contested between the Goths and the Byzantines. In 541-44 the latter erected a secondary city wall inside the old Roman city but in 552 even this failed to keep out the Goth, Totila. The new city walls were built utilizing the structures of various large Roman buildings: the Campidoglio, the reservoir for the water of the Baths, the Theater. A pair of coupled towers, whose foundations have recently come to light behind the remains of the side apses of Santa Reparata, terminated the fortifications of the small «Byzantine» city wall at the northeast corner. The wall was trapezoidal and its modest size testifies to the decline of the city, greatly depopulated (there may have been less than a thousand inhabitants) and reduced to a *castrum*. Meanwhile, in the early decades of the 6th century or even before, but certainly at the time of the late Roman city, the church of **Santa Reparata** was built. According to tradition, and this includes Villani, the Florentines built the church in 405, a tribute to the victory of General Stilicho's imperial troops over the Ostrogoths of Radagaisus. Recent excavations have shown that the church was built as a basilica, with a nave and two aisles separated by columns and with a single apse. The pavement, of which only part remains, was composed of a pattern of large rectangular compartments, with mosaic decorations of various motifs and geometric interlacing. At the center, a compartment with a peacock, symbol of immortality, bore the name of one of the donors «OBSEQUENTIUS FECIT PED. XXX». Other religious buildings were added onto the list of churches of the Roman period during Byzantine rule (552-568): Santa Maria Odigitria, later called *Santa Maria in Campidoglio* because it was on the site of the Temple to the Capitoline Triad, *San Ruffillo* and *Sant'Apollinaire*. Around the end of the 6th century when the Lombards conquered northern and central Italy, Florence also fell under their dominion. This was the beginning of what may be considered the darkest period in the city's history. Cut off from the major routes, the main reason for its existence suddenly vanished. For their north-south communications, the Lombards abandoned the central Bologna-Pistoia-Florence route as being too exposed to the incursions of the Byzantines who still held control of Romania, and made use of a route further to the west that crossed the Cisa pass and reached Pavia and Milan via the Sarzana-Piacenza route.

In the Middle Ages this road, later to be known as *romea* or *francigena*, became the main continental artery between Italy and the countries north of the Alps. Similar reasons lie behind the Lombard choice of Lucca as the capital of the duchy of Toscana, a city that lay along the road they used for internal communications.

In any case, during the period of Lombard domination, especially after Queen Theodolinda had been converted to the church of Rome, a number of religious buildings were founded in the city: *San Salvatore* (its location is uncertain), *San Giorgio*, *Sant'Andrea «in Foro Vetere»*, *San Pietro in Ciel d'Oro* (so-called because the apse was probably decorated with gold mosaics), *San Miniato tra le Torri*, *San Pier Maggiore* and *Santa Maria de «Ferlaupe»*, part of which still

A stretch of the Roman fullery uncovered by the archaeological excavations in the Piazza della Signoria.

remains under the pavement of the church of *San Piero Scheraggio*, now part of the building of the *Uffizi*. A tradition which was never abandoned and which comes down to us from the earliest Florentine chronicles, also ties the building of the *Baptistery of San Giovanni* in with the conversion of Queen Theodolinda, although not of course in its present form and size. Indeed it seems that the original Florentine baptismal church was much smaller than the present one: it was most likely a small octagonal temple whose foundations are visible in the «subterraneans» of «bel San Giovanni».

Various facts seem to testify to a revival of the city in Carolingian times. The measure undertaken by Emperor Lothair I to reunite Florence and Fiesole into a single county, for instance, dates to 854. The count of Florence, a title acquired by the Marquis of Tuscia, had jurisdiction over a vast province which embraced the territories of two dioceses. Even if the two provinces were later restored, the fact indicates a tendency on the part of Florence to enlarge its territorial jurisdiction at the expense of nearby Fiesole, which, in those same years, seems to have had the western part of its diocese curtailed and annexed to the territory of the Florentine diocese. In the 9th century a public ecclesiastic school was established in the city, and the bridge over the Arno, which had been destroyed during the Gotho-Byzantine war, seems to have been rebuilt. Moreover at the turn of the century new city walls were built, probably for fear of Hungarian invasions. The new walls, the third set, partly followed the line of the old Roman walls, widening on the south to enclose the suburbs (*borghi*) which had grown up in the direction of the Arno (a sign that the city had grown), while to the north, for political reasons, the *Baptistery, Santa Reparata*, the *Bishop's palace* as well as the adjacent *palatium regis* where the Emperor's representative held his «court of justice», were excluded.

Towards the end of the 10th century, Countess Willa, widow of the Marquis of Tuscany, Uberto, who owned an entire district within the walls, founded and richly endowed a Benedictine abbey in memory of her husband. It was dedicated to *Santa Maria Assunta in Cielo* and the monastic complex was later simply to be known as **Badia Fiorentina** for it was and continued to be the ideal municipal monastery. Countess Willa's son, Hugo, greatly contributed to the development of Florence thanks to his decision to leave Lucca. His choice of the city on the banks of the Arno as his dwelling place reinforced its administrative character. The reconstruction of the church and monastery of **San Miniato al Monte** was another sign of the city's recovery. Work was begun in 1013 by Bishop Hildebrand, encouraged and financially aided by Emperor Henry II and his wife Cunegonda. The church, expression of the devotion of the Florentines to their saint, had ancient origins. A document dated April 30, 783, already mentions it as an important abbey to which Emperor Charlemagne donated lands and houses in suffrage of his beloved bride Hildegard who died when she was only 26 years old. Apparently however both the church and the monastery were almost totally destroyed and the building Bishop Hildebrand consecrated on April 27, 1018 was completely new and was defined as *decenter constructum* in a successive document of 1062.

Remains of the Church of S. Piero Scheraggio in Via della Ninna.

EARLY MIDDLE AGES

Around the middle of the 11th century the position of Florence in Tuscany became even more important because Lucca was no longer the seat of the marquisate and because of the city's decisive participation in the movement for the reform of the church. The struggle to eliminate secular interference in ecclesiastical affairs and the affirmation of the independence of the papacy from imperial power were to have their leading representative in San Giovanni Gualberto, the son of a Florentine knight, who founded the order of Vallombrosa. In 1055 Florence even played host to a council, under Pope Victor II with the presence of Emperor Henry III and the participation of 120 bishops. It is not unlikely that the occasion (of the Council) prompted the enlargement or partial reconstruction of the cathedral of **Santa Reparata**. It may already have been altered in the early Middle Ages and was certainly brought up to date in the 11th century. As recent excavations have shown, the Romanesque church was characterized by a thoroughly Lombardian gravity in the row of powerful square piers which divided the interior into three wide aisles. The presbytery was raised and had a large crypt underneath. The plan of the early Florentine cathedral as then established consisted of three aisles which led to a large central apse flanked by two smaller ones and two arms, also with apses, which opened off the sides.

Other old structures were also rebuilt during the second half of the 11th century: the *Baptistery, Santa Felicita, San Lorenzo, San Pier Maggiore, San Remigio* and the *Santi Apostoli*. On November 6, 1059, Bishop Gerard, who had become pope under the name of Nicholas II, reconsecrated the ancient baptismal chuch of the city which had been rebuilt in more imposing form, much like what it is today. The building, octagonal in plan, with a semicircular apse on one side and three entrances, seems to have been covered by a pointed-arch dome divided into eight sectors. The outside was not yet faced with its fine marble casing, but inside it presumably already had the trabeation, at least on the lower level, which rhythmically scans the sides of the polygon. The two porphyry columns presented to the Florentines by the Pisans as thanks for the services they rendered Pisa during the Balearic enterprise did not arrive until 1117, too late to be used. After the death of her mother and of her husband (Geoffrey the Bearded), Matilda, daughter of Countess Beatrice, became the sole countess of Tuscany. She had always adhered to the ideas of the Reform and the policies of San Giovanni Gualberto and during the struggle for investiture she gave her support to the most influential of the reformers, Hildebrand of Sovana who later became Pope Gregory VII, thus finding herself in open contrast with the emperor, Henry IV. After the episode of Canossa, Henry IV's victory in 1081 led to the official deposition of the Countess who was abandoned by all the Tuscan cities except Florence. This faithfulness to the deposed Countess cost the city an imperial siege in July of 1082 (the first important military action the Florentine city was involved in) which however failed.

Matilda's special attachment to Florence and the consequent rupture with the emperor led to the construction, in 1078, of a more efficient system of defense and the city was supplied with new walls - those which Dante was to call «*la cerchia antica*». This fourth walled enclosure for the most part followed along the lines of the Carolingian walls but on the north included the *Baptistery*, the cathedral of *Santa Reparata* and the residence of the Countess. The course of the 11th century walls can still be seen clearly in the urban layout: from the «*Castello di Altafronte*» (now *Palazzo de' Giudici*), set on the Arno, the walls followed the alignment of Via dei Castellani, Via dei Leoni, Piazza San Firenze and Via del Proconsolo, then turning west towards what is now Piazza del Duomo, and continuing along Via dei Cerretani, Via Rondinelli and Via Tornabuoni, as far as the church of Santa Trinita, at which point it once more turned and followed a route parallel to the course of the Arno along the line Borgo Santi Apostoli - Via Lambertesca, returning to *Castello d'Altafronte*. The course of the Mugnone was moved to the south so that it could serve as a moat for the walls on the western side and the stream ran into the Arno approximately where the bridge of Santa Trinita now is.

In this period the city was divided into quarters which took their names from the four main gates: the *Porta San Piero* on the east, the so-called «*Porta del vescovo*» to the north, the *Porta San Pancrazio* to the west and the *Porta Santa Maria* to the south. Remembrances of the fourth gate are still to be found in the city's toponymy as in *Via Por Santa Maria* or *Via Porta Rossa* which took its name from a postern or secondary gate in the southwest corner and which was called *Porta Rossa* because it was built of brick.

Like all the early medieval cities, the town plan of 11th-century Florence must have been characterized not only by the recovery of its antique urban structure (walls, various remnants of roads) but by a basic homogenity, expressed in a casual distribution of the various landmarks. There were probably no open public spaces of any great size, with the exception of the market areas, the largest of which occupied the site of the ancient *forum*; the squares documented near the main churches were probably simply extensions. The urban fabric must have been composed primarily of wooden houses and only an occasional tower-house in stone set on the foundations of a Roman building loomed up against the sky. The principal landmarks were doubtless the religous buildings: besides the *Baptistery* and *Santa Reparata* and the other old establishments, several churches stood outside the city walls along the roads that led away from the gates: *San Pier Maggiore, Santo Stefano al Ponte, Sant'Apollinare, Santa Maria Novella, San Felice*, the church of the *Santo Sepolcro*, etc.

Some of the religious buildings mentioned above were renovated during the 11th century and were the earliest examples of the Florentine Romanesque style characterized by a particular fidelity to antiquity. According to Argan's intriguing hypothesis «the doctrinal orientation of the intense religious life of the city» might provide a reliable explanation for Florentine classicism. The thesis, of Benedictine origin, affirmed in the 11th century cultural ambit, was that any logical discussion of «Truth, which is, in itself, rational and the demonstration of which is implicit in the clarity of the enunciation, of the form» was superfluous. An artistic concept which demanded that architecture express itself in clear geometric forms capable of revealing their rational basis with immediacy was thus born. The building which, *par excellence*, expressed this preference for geometric forms and for the definition of spatial values was the *Baptistery* which was to be of enormous importance for the history of the figurative arts in Florence. San Giovanni became a sort of paradigmatic exposition of the Florentine concept of architecture, bound in so many ways to a classical idea of space, seen as form rather than force.

THE PERIOD OF THE COMMUNES

At the death of Countess Matilda (1115) the Florentine populace to all effects already constituted a Commune. The numerous privileges conceded by the *«gran contessa»* and the events in which the Florentine community had played a leading role in the struggle against the emperor, induced the people to organize autonomously and to undertake action aimed at weakening imperial power. It was therefore inevitable that in 1125, upon the death of the last emperor of the Franconian dynasty, Henry V, the Florentines decided to attack and destroy Fiesole, the neighboring rival city. As a result the two counties were conclusively united and remained as separate entities only on an ecclesiastic level with Fiesole maintaining its own diocese. In any case Fiesole as a city was annulled and, no more nor less than the suburbs of the *contado*, was obliged to acknowledge Florentine supremacy with the symbolic offering of candles at the Baptistery for the festivities of St. John the Baptist.

The first mention of an officially constituted Commune dates to 1138. Two Florentine consuls, Brocardus and Selvorus, are mentioned as representatives of the city in a meeting of the Tuscan cities held at San Genesio (on the *via pisana* where it crossed with the *via francigena*) and where it was decided to constitute a League, for fear that Henry the Proud who had in precedence oppressed them as imperial legate might be elected emperor. From the middle of the 12th century on, information about the political make-up of the Commune became more specific. We are thus informed that it was under the guidance of twelve consuls, who took turns, two at a time, every two months. They were flanked by a council of *boni homines*, consisting of 100-150 individuals, while at the base was the popular assembly or Parliament, which met four times a year in the cathedral of *Santa Reparata*.

From what we can gather from the documents, the social structure of the city reveals a community constituted of religious and secular representatives, with three dominant social groups: the nobles, grouped into *consorterie* (the so-called *«Società delle torri»*), the merchants, and the horse soldiers, the backbone of the army, who included all those, noble or not, who were able to provide their own arms and on horseback serve the militia of the Commune. Among the nobles were to be found the old feudal families who had always lived in the city such as the Uberti and the Adimari, as well as the landed proprieters of the surrounding countryside or *contado* who were forced to live within the walls once they had been conquered by the Commune. Examples were the Buondelmonti and the Ubaldini. Although the nobles held most of the power in the 12th century, it was nevertheless mainly the merchants who were responsible for the growth of the city. The rise of the merchants accellerated in the second half of the century, as trade with distant countries was intensified and became a new and much richer source for the accumulation of capital. Extensive trade and its inseparable companion, credit, were what provided the Commune with its power of growth and were the basis for the economic and demographic expansion of the city.

The requisites of commercial activity (the need for free circulation of the goods that arrived in or left from Florence) forced the Commune to protect the communication routes from the extravagant tolls imposed by the proprieters of the *contado*, as well as the authority of the neighboring municipalities. Throughout the 12th century therefore a goodly part of the military power of the Commune was earmarked for the struggle against the feudal regime (represented above all by the *consorterie* bound to the noble Guidi and Alberti families) and against rival Communes. The stages in the progressive expansion of Florentine control over its own *contado* were marked by the demolition of the feudal castles, which surrounded the city in what might almost be called concentric circles. In 1107 the castle of Monte Orlando near Gangalandi fell. It belonged to the Cadolingi. In 1110 the castle the Alberti counts owned near Cerbaia, in Val di Pesa, was razed to the ground. In 1113 another Cadolingi fortress, at Monte Cascioli, near Castelpulci, was demolished. In 1135 Montebuoni, headquarters of the Buondelmonti, was destroyed, and in the same year the castle of Montegufoni in Val di Pesa, property of the Ormanni family, was torn down. In 1142 the castle of Quona, in the vicinity of Pontassieve, belonging to the Guidi counts, was wiped out. In 1154 they also lost the castle of Monte Croce, near Fiesole. In 1176 the castle of Montegrossoli, in the Chianti region, property of the Firidolfi, and that of Pogne, in Valdelsa, property of the Alberti counts were eliminated. In 1184 the castle of Mangona, near Barberino di Mugello, one of the most powerful fortresses which also belonged to the Alberti family, was taken.

This process of expansion underwent a temporary halt when Frederick Barbarossa advanced south into Italy. In 1185 the emperor even deprived the city of its *contado* and restored the marquisate of Tuscany, setting his younger son Philip at its head. But the provision had a brief life. In 1197, taking advantage of the death of Barbarossa's successor, Henry VI, Florence regained control of her *contado*, which she had probably never completely lost. At the end of the century and at the beginning of the 13th century, thanks to a series of fortunate military exploits, the Florentine Commune succeeded in getting most of the peoples of the *contado* to pledge allegiance «which formerly had been owed to the signoria of the counts of Guidi and those of Mangona and Capraia and Certaldo». (G. Villani, Cronica, V, 21). Henceforws, deprived of their authority and their power, were to be pushed back to the borders of the municipal territory and later fought and defeated even in what was left of their dominions.

The rivalry with the neighboring municipalities also led to any number of disputes, mostly based on pretexts involving the establishment of boundaries of their respective spheres of competence. Particularly frequent was conflict with Siena, which was enlarging its *contado* in southern Tuscany at the expense of the border-

An old picture showing the Mercato Vecchio and the Column of Plenty before the opening up of the Piazza della Repubblica.

ing cities. With Pisa, which was the richest city in the western Mediterranean in the 12th century, things were different. Since Florence normally used the port of Pisa for its commerce with overseas countries, their relationship was one of collaboration and mutual aid. Clear evidence of the power Florence had acquired in the course of the 12th century is to be found in the expansion of its urban territory. All around the circle of Matilda's walls, in correspondence to the gates, populous suburbs had sprung up, initially elongated in form as they flanked the streets that ran out of the city. Even now the city's toponymy preserves their memory: Borgo San Lorenzo, in reference to the Porta del Vescovo; Borgo di Balla (the name of the first stretch of what is now the Via dei Servi, for this was where the *tiratori* or wool dryers of the Wool Guild were located and there was therefore an intense traffic of bales (*balle*) of wool); Borgo San Pier Maggiore; Borgo de' Greci (so called because of the presence of a colony of eastern traders); Borgo San Remigio; Borgo di Porta Santa Maria; etc. Not to mention the agglomerates which had risen on the other side of the Arno: Borgo San Jacopo. Borgo di Piazza (now Via Guicciardini), Borgo «Pidiglioso» (corresponding to what is now the Via dei Bardi), its name based on the fact, according to Villani, that it was inhabited by «vile gente». In 1172 the Commune therefore decided to enlarge the city walls and incorporate the newest districts. The perimeter of the new city walls, raised in barely two years (from 1173 to 1175), was twice that of the «old circle» and enclosed an area that was three times as great. The new walls touched on the Arno and were characterized by a rotation of about 45° with respect to the other city walls which had all been basically planned in relation to the Roman quadrilateral. As a result each side of the old belt (and the gates which generally were set at the center) corresponded to a corner of the new walls. Thus after more than a thousand years, the orientation of the city and its network of streets finally corresponded with the layout of the various routes enclosing the city which were based on the division into *centuriae* of the land surrounding the Roman colony. The course of the Mugnone was once more deviated for the construction of the new city walls. Brought further west, it flowed into the moats that ran along the walls, reminiscences of which are found in the names of what is now the Via dei Fossi (moats), as well as the church of *San Jacopo tra i Fossi*, in what is now the Via dei Benci. In place of the traditional four entrances, the new enclosure had six main gates and four posterns. As far as the suburbs across the Arno were concerned, which initially lacked an organic system of defence, it was not until later that they were fortified, even though a small part of the «Oltrarno» was enclosed in the walls as early as 1173-1175. As a result the Arno became an infrastructure within the city, both as a communications route as well as a source of energy and a water supply for industries (mills and fulling mills). The bridge over the river, rebuilt in the early Middle Ages, «fell at the end of the fourth day of November» and was rebuilt at the present site of *Ponte Vecchio*, but with five arches and a road surface that was not nearly as wide as it is today.

In the 12th century the urban fabric of the city must have been punctuated by numerous towers: in 1180 thirty-five were documented, but there were certainly many more. The existence of the towers, however, did not establish a «logical order coordinated by environ-

mental and monumental qualifications» since basically their distribution was not bound to any special part, neither the «*civitas vetus*» (the Roman, Carolingian and Matildan city) nor the «*civitas nova*». Originally the purpose of the towers was that of offense and defense. They provided the owners with a place of refuge in case of danger and were therefore built alongside the houses with which they communicated through openings in the adjoining walls. Only later were the towers used as houses (13th-14th centuries) when they underwent a series of transformations giving them the form we know from surviving examples: the **Visdomini tower** in the Via delle Oche, the **Baldovinetti tower** in the Borgo Santi Apostoli, the **Torre della Castagna**, in the Piazza San Martino del Vescovo. The tower-houses were not as high as they had previously been, and were provided with more openings and had large portals with pointed arch moldings at the base (previously the only entrance, as specified above, had been at a certain height). But in the 12th century the towers still served for military purposes and gave birth to the phenomenon of the «Tower Societies», associations which reunited the owners of various towers and through which an association (or *consorteria*) of sev-

This page and facing page: two old tower-houses still standing in the city center.

eral noble families succeeded in controlling a portion of the city. This union of various towers into the same association lies at the base of the city block, a typical structural unit of urban space in the 12th century.

A considerable number of small and large churches also sprang up as the size of the city increased. In two centuries the number of churches in Florence was tripled, so that at the beginning of the 13th century the city had as many as 48 churches (12 priories and 36 parishes). The *Codex* of Marco di Bartolomeo Rustici, which dates to the end of the Middle Ages (mid-15th century) shows us the architectural features of those churches which have since disappeared or been totally transformed (*Santa Maria in Campidoglio, San Michele in Palchetto, San Bartolommeo, San Leo, San Martino del Vescovo*, etc.). In only a few cases have the extant buildings preserved more or less conspicuous parts of their original Romanesque structure: besides the most important examples which will be discussed later, see the crypt and the interior facade of the church of **Santa Trinita**, the facade and the two flanks of **Santa Maria Maggiore**, some of the piers and capitals formerly in **Santa Felicita**, the crypt of **San Niccolò**, the cylindrical base of the **campanile of the Badia**, the divisory piers

between the nave and aisles of **San Jacopo sopr'Arno** (in front of the facade is the recomposed Romanesque portico of the extraurban church of San Donato in Scopeto), the small facade of **San Salvatore al Vescovo**, the small churches of **Santa Margherita de' Cerchi** and **Santi Procolo e Diomede**.

The 12th century was to be the scene for intensive building activity which led to the reconstruction of all the extant churches and the creation of new religious buildings in the suburbs which had sprung up around the old walls. With the exception of the simplest little churches (modest chapels to be identified by an oculus on the facade and a small openwork supporting structure for the bells), all the main buildings (or what remains) reflect the specific features of the Florentine Romanesque which were already present as noted in the earliest manifestations of the 11th- century architectural renewal. In **San Miniato al Monte** and in **San Piero Scheraggio** the classicizing aspects (colonnades, wooden rafter ceilings) fuse with elements borrowed from the Lombard Romanesque (multiple piers, transversal arches). Sometimes, as in the church of the **Santi Apostoli**, the use of classicizing modes was accentuated even more: the continuous colonnades in the interior, without the Lombardian interruptions in the rhythms, and the Corinthian capitals, closely relate the building to early Christian architecture.

In the 12th century the administration of two of the most important churches in the city (the *Baptistery* and *San Miniato al Monte*) was entrusted to the Consuls of the wealthiest of the Florentine Guilds, the *Arte di Calimala*. As a result the two buildings were subjected to numerous transformations from which their present aspect is derived. Most probably the marble revetments of the first two orders on the exterior of the **Baptistery** date to the second half of the 12th century. The designs of the two-color facing in inlays of green serpentine on white marble, which was sometimes reused, are wonderfully suited to the clarity of the building's structure. Each face of the octagon was divided by engaged pilaster strips topped by a trabeation and articulated above by blind arcades into which edicule windows with triangular or curved pediments were inscribed. These are clearly adaptations of classic models, reinterpreted however with an originality that expresses itself in terms of graceful elegance. The motive of the rectangular window surmounted by the triangle of the pediment, in particular, was later to be extremely popular in the architecture of Florence. A row of stylized loggias in recollection of Lombard taste was inserted between the blind arcading and the trabeated engaged pilasters. But since the loggias were solely inlaid they were reduced to a pure graphic symbol. Inside, on the other hand, the *Baptistery* preserved its sober and severe ornamental scheme which was probably contemporary with the building. The space is enclosed in a sort of cage formed of two trabeations between which the system of pilasters, columns and engaged pilaster strips which articulate the faces of the octagon rises up.

Except for the bottom part of the facade, the church furnishings and most of the external and interior marble facing of **San Miniato** date back to the second half of the 12th century (or the early decades of the 13th century). The original construction consecrated in 1018 by Bishop Hildebrand was later radically transformed, resulting in the present building which, despite certain Lombard reminiscences, is the expression of a

15

The simple facade of the Church of S. Maria Maggiore.

tive ensemble of the facade harmoniously completes the architecture, especially in the lower parts, realizing a perfect equilibrium between the architectural structures and the marble incrustation, in line with the parameters of the artistic culture dominant in 12th-century Florence, generally described as being «geometric» both in the «formal as well as operative-deductive or rational sense of the term» (C.L. Ragghianti). Every element in the decoration thus becomes a sort of projection on a plane of the architectural structures, beginning with the basic arcades which develop in a slow solemn rhythm, circumscribing the portals and the marble surfaces, and almost seem to repeat the cadences of a portico. But on the whole, the other inlaid ornamental motifs also refer to three-dimensional details, presenting, in graphic form, rose windows, loggias, portals, fretwork.

When the new city walls went up and the urban space was enlarged, the city was also reorganized from the administrative point of view, and was divided into six quarters or districts, three of which corresponded to the old quarters which had spread out as far as the new walls (San Pancrazio, Porta Duomo and San Piero Scheraggio); two others were the result of the division in two parts, «come vae la maestra strada», of the neighborhood of Por Santa Maria, which became the two districts of Borgo Santi Apostoli and of Por Santa Maria. The sixth was the district on the other side of the Arno (Oltrarno). This new division of the city corresponded to a new administrative ordinance of the country district as well, where the division into districts according to the *plebati* was maintained, at the same time reuniting the people into six large circumscriptions, each of which fell under an urban sixth quarter, which testifies clearly to the fact that the rural territory was under complete control.

new architectural concept, the fruit of an original fusion with the late antique tradition. The church has three wide aisles separated by columns, which, in a rhythm of a a b, alternate with polystyle piers from which the transverse arches which subdivide the nave into three bays spring. The last of these forms the presbytery with its apse. Raised with respect to the rest of the church and closed off by marble transennas, the presbytery lies over a crypt divided into seven aisles with cross vaults set on marble columns. The capitals of the columns and of the piers, mostly Corinthian, in part come from monuments of antiquity, others are of Romanesque manufacture, but modelled on the antique. Some of the latter are in terracotta rather than marble like the others. Composite in type, with the flower and the abacus in sandstone, they are similar to those still visible in what remains of *San Piero Schieraggio*. The marble decoration of the interior is original only on the back wall and the side walls of the presbytery as far as the trabeation. All the rest (including the casing of the columns in polychrome scagliola in imitation marble) dates to the restorative integrations of the 19th century. The classic spirit comes to the fore in this decoration where the alternation of white and dark green marble clearly distinguishes the geometric surfaces with geometric inlays of precisely calculated proportions. In the casing of the curve of the apse, however, the blind arcades which circumscribe the three niche-windows filled with slabs of red fangite echo the motifs which came from north of the Alps, despite the use of a classical framework. The decora-

THE THIRTEENTH CENTURY

The speed with which the new walls were built is a sign of the prosperity that reigned in Florence. The city had become the principal center of continental Tuscany, with a population that at this point must have been around 30,000 inhabitants, and which clearly showed signs of continued growth thanks to the arrival of immigrants from the countryside. This immigration from the *contado*, consisting prevalently of the more well-to-do classes, gave rise to a new middle class, an important factor in the tensions which accompanied the struggles between the nobles who held the power and all those others who were excluded, including the majority of commoners. In 1193 the tensions flared up and some of the important noble families (including the Uberti) which up to then had been kept at a distance from the consulate, backed by the favor of the emperor, took over the government. Basically the new ruling group was not unlike the old group, from a social point of view. The difference was mainly rappresented by the passage to a regime centered on a podestà, in which the executive power was entrusted to a single magistrate known as «Podestà». But with the death of Henry VI (1197), the families who had been ousted returned to favor and the consular system was reestablished. But not for long, for under the joint pressure of the social categories that were still excluded from power (shopkeepers, artisans), the regime of podestà was definitely installed in 1207, with the Podestà a foreigner (the first was Gualfredotto da Milano) so as to guarantee impartiality in the application of the law. The Podestà was flanked by a small council which replaced the Collegio dei Consoli, and by a Consiglio Generale, which included representatives of the merchants, so that the new system of government, which balanced the opposing tendencies of the noble ruling classes, was also accessible in part to the middle classes.

The Commune thus experienced a period of peace during which the economic basis of the city continued to expand. The merchants, who had begun to organize in corporate association (the *Arte dei Mercanti*) in 1182, on the example of the Society of Knights, multiplied and spread well beyond the limits of their region. Around the turn of the century Florence thus became an international economic center, with its operators in the principal fairs of the West. The development of the economy went on at such a rate that in a few years the associations multiplied among the other categories of tradesmen and artisans, whose number increased considerably. The *Arte dei Mercanti* or Merchants' Guild in particular became more important. It began to be called *Arte di Calimala*, from the name of the stretch of street where the shops specialized in refinishing and dying the woolen cloths that had been imported in unfinished form from the other side of the Alps were located. These woolens were then resold in all the main markets of the West. The city still preserves some of the buildings which served as headquarters for the Guilds. Generally they are buildings which date back to the 14th century, such as the **headquarters of the Wool Guild** (*Arte della Lana*), built in 1308 by restructuring an extant tower, and restored with integrations in style in the 19th century, or the **residence of the Arte dei Beccai** (Butchers' Guild), in the Via Orsanmichele. In various cases howeve the ancient seats of the Guilds were destroyed, especially with the demolition of the old city center: this is what happened for instance to the residence of the *Arte dei Rigattieri e Linaioli* and that of the *Albergatori*.

The increase in size and population, due not to a natural increment but to the accellerated immigration from the countryside, lay at the basis of this economic expansion. The immigrants, members of a rural middle class that had been formed in consequence of the general economic development, settled in the city district which corresponded to the part of the *contado* from which they came. This was why the Oltrarno, on which the populous southern regions converged, increased enormously and this was why a new bridge in wood on stone piers (called *Ponte alla Carraia*) was constructed (1128) downstream from the extant bridge which then took the name of *Vecchio*. A few years later (1237) a third bridge was built upstream, taking its name from the Podestà in office at the time, Rubaconte da Mondello from Milan. This bridge, completely in stone, was set across the widest point of the Arno. Originally it consisted of as many as nine arches but two were closed in 1347 so as to enlarge the Piazza dei Mozzi. Later its name was changed to *Ponte alle Grazie*, after the small church which was built on one of its piers in the middle of the 14th century, and which was then flanked by various small shops and a number of small

Above: the headquarters of the Arte della Lana (Wool Guild) and, below, the headquarters of the Arte dei Beccai (Butchers' Guild).

houses in which cloistered nuns lived. The pressing needs of trade and commerce between the cities, the result of the urban expansion, led to the construction in 1952 of still another bridge across the Arno: the *Ponte a Santa Trinita*. The four bridges served the city's needs up to the 19th century, although in 1317, the construction of a fifth bridge was begun in honor of King Robert of Naples and in expectation of further growth on the part of the city (which did not occur). The bridge, known as *Ponte Reale* and situated somewhat downstream from the present Ponte San Niccolò, was never finished and in 1532 Duke Alessandro de' Medici used its foundations for the erection of a fort on the Arno. With the exception of the Ponte alle Grazie, all the other bridges were destroyed in the disastrous flood of 1333. Even so, after their reconstruction, they maintained their typically medieval character with small buildings serving a variety of purposes erected on their structures.

The concentration of population in Florence and the profound religious sense of its inhabitants obviously attracted the mendicant orders, the expression of the renewed 13th-century spirituality. The new religious orders (Franciscan, Dominican, Augustinian, Servite, Carmelite) played a leading role in the structuralization of the late medieval city. Since their apostolates required densely populated areas and large spaces where they could meet with the citizenry, they erected vast convent complexes and became poles of attraction which grew up side by side with the linear routes of the suburbs in organizing the activity and life of entire sectors of the urban area. The history of the architecture of the mendicant orders in Florence can be divided more or less into two periods. The first, from the origins up to the middle of the 13th century, witnessed the foundation of the communities and the construction of the first churches, all buildings of modest size as counselled for example by the *Dominican Constitutions* of 1240, cited almost integrally by the Franciscans: «*Mediocres domos et humiles habeant fratres nostri...*». Later, when the mendicant orders had acquired prestige within the 13th-century society, the increasingly intense activity in the field of preaching and religious instruction of the people necessitated enlarging the first small constructions. This was the beginning of the second period in Franciscan and Dominican architectural history, as well as that of all the other mendicant orders, which witnessed the *ex-novo* construction, often in grandiose form, of most of the original buildings. The Dominicans, who had established themselves in Florence in 1221 in the small church of *Santa Maria delle Vigne*, which had been donated by the cathedral chapter, enlarged the original heart of their monastery for the first time in 1246 and then in 1278 began the present structure. The first church of the Franciscans, dedicated to the *Holy Cross* (*Santa Croce*) dates to the second quarter of the 13th century. At the end of the century (1295) it was rebuilt as we see it today. And the same thing happened with the Agostinians of *Santo Spirito*, who established themselves in the heart of the Oltrarno in 1259 and a few years later (1296) enlarged their monastery; with the Carmelites of *Santa Maria del Carmine*; the Servites of the *Santissima Annunziata*, a mendicant order which originated in Florence.

Even in the diversity of their formal solutions, the religious structures of the new orders were all characterized by the grandness of their buildings, due in part to the religious requirements (the need for large spaces to house the faithful and instruct them with the Word, and with the frescoed images on the large well-lit walls) and in part to the fact that the churches were considered real public buildings, built by the people and for the people «*ad utilitatem animarum et decorum civitatis expedit*». In addition to restructuring the precedent churches, the new religious organism created vast convent complexes, full of cloisters and rooms for study and work; they organized the communitarian life of the urban population, playing a role in political and cultural as well as religious life.

The intense building activity of the mendicant orders was paralleled by the renewal of various city churches, beginning with the Vallombrosan *Santa Trinita* rebuilt in Gothic forms between 1250 and 1260. Two convents were founded in the locality known as Cafaggio: the convent of *Santa Maria degli Angioli* (1295), by the monks of Camaldoli, and the monastery of *San Marco* (1299) by the Silvestrini fathers. The *Badia Fiorentina* was also enlarged (1285) by Arnolfo di Cambio, and various churches were renewed: *Santo Stefano al Ponte* (1233), *San Simone* (1243), *Santa Maria Maggiore, Sant'Ambrogio*. Lastly between 1278 and 1294, the Umiliati friars, who had come to Florence from Alexandria in 1239 and had initially settled near San Donato a Torri, built with their monastery the church of *San Salvatore in Ognissanti*, transferring their workshops for the working of wool, in which they were masters, to the city as well.

The practice of charity which together with prayer was one of the fundamentals of the religious creed of the new congregations, stimulated the foundation of new hospitals alongside the older ones, some of which are mentioned as early as the 11th century (such as the *Spedale di Badia*, the *Spedale dei Pinti*, near the church of *San Pier Maggiore*, and that of the *Santo Sepolcro*, on the other side of the *Ponte Vecchio*). Among the numerous hospitals which rose during the 13th or early in the 14th century mention must be made at least of the *Spedale of Santa Maria Nuova*, founded by Folco Portinari in 1286, which was later to become the principal hospital of the city, as well as the *hospital of San Matteo* in the Piazza San Marco (of which the Gothic loggia remains), and that of *San Martino alla Scala*, later transformed into a convent.

Together with the new cathedral of *Santa Maria del Fiore*, whose construction began in 1294, the large churches erected by the mendicant orders in the last decades of the 13th century constituted the principal examples of Gothic religious architecture in Florence. The new forms, imported into Italy by the Cistercians (who had built the Badia a Settimo, at the gates of the city, in the first half of the 13th century), fused on the Arno with the classicizing taste and geometric two-color decoration which characterizes the tradition of Florentine architecture. The result was an original interpretation of the Gothic, in which the accentuated asending movement of the churches north of the Alps was moderated in a more measured and perfectly finished concept of space.

In **Santa Maria Novella**, traditionally attributed to the Dominicans Fra Sisto and Fra Ristoro, the vast bare interior with a tripartite nave, realized with humble materials (*pietra serena* in the piers and ribs, brickwork pavement, plastered walls and vaulting) has a clearly defined stylistic character thanks to the sharp silhouetting of the structural framework against the clear

The soaring bell tower of the Badia.

expanses of the masses of masonry and to the limpid proportions of the space in which there seems to be an expansion of linear impulse from the nave to the aisles. In **Santa Croce**, attributed to Arnolfo di Cambio, the vertical thrust of the northern churches is even more attenuated in «the clear pulsing of the spaces and the lucid legibility of the individual parts». The nave is separated from the aisles by slender octagonal columns from which the broad pointed arches with their double moldings spring. The ceiling, according to the Franciscan rule, is an open timber roof so that the space is presented as a volume in which the verticality of the linear profiles is continuously set in relation to the horizontal elements, represented by the ceiling and the balcony below, accentuating the perspective which leads towards the open luminous central apse with its high windows.

In the course of the 13th century various modifications were effectuated on the **Baptistery**, bringing it closer to its present shape. In 1202 the semicircular apse was replaced by the rectangular tribune (*scarsella*). A few years later (1225) the tribune was decorated with mosaics by Fra Jacopo «*Sancti Francisci frater*» and still later the grandiose mosaic decoration of the dome was begun. The work was entrusted to the «Greek masters» (as Vasari called them) with the collaboration of local artists such as Cimabue and Gaddo Gaddi, and continued intermittently for a century. In the second half of the 13th century the upper story of the marble decoration of the exterior was added, as well as the pyramidal roof which concealed the dome and was felicitously engrafted to the octagonal prism below it. The new decorative band is marked by the sober two-color geometric inlays and the faint relief of the pilaster strips which are distinguished from the background almost solely because of their contrasting color. The white marble slabs of the perfectly smooth pyramid roof stress the volume of the building which in its upper part gives the effect of being a sort of *templum cristallinum*. The lightness of the decorative system of the exterior must have been even more evident before the corners were reinforced and encased in horizontal marble stripes (1293) which contrast with the rhythm of the pilasters supporting the blind arcading as well as with the function of the corners which were meant to frame the surfaces and not to serve as areas of transition.

THE STRUGGLES BETWEEN THE GUELPHS AND THE GHIBELLINES

The period of peace which followed the installation of government under a podestà did not last long. As early as 1216 the antagonism between the *consorterie* of the Buondelmonte and the Amidei served as a pretext for a renewal of the struggles within the ruling group and for the beginning of feuds which were to afflict Florentine society for the entire century, dividing the citizens between Guelphs and Ghibellines. In 1244 the Ghibelline nobles, who were in power, decided to broaden the social base of the government, so as to obtain the favor of the merchant middle class. This was the prelude to the beginning of the period that was to be known as «Primo Popolo». The Podestà was flanked by two «Captains», representatives of the «People», that is of the organizations of commerce and the artisans. But only a few years later (1250) the merchants and the artisans as a whole, «radunandosi insieme a romore», managed to usurp the power of the Ghibelline nobles and initiate a new political policy. The «Popolo» was juxtaposed to the other municipal institutions. The new organization was of a military character: twenty companies based on a topographical distribution each had their own banner, gonfalonier and Council. The «Capitano del Popolo» was set at its head. To ensure his impartiality he was to be a foreigner and he was flanked by a Council of ancients and a Council of the representatives of the Guilds.

The *Societas militum* were abolished, in the hopes of allaying the arrogance of the nobles and of preventing them from returning to power. So all the towers had to be cut down to a height of 50 *braccia* (29 meters), «... since (the city) had a great quantity 120 *braccia* high». This was the beginning of another period of peace and prosperity and the city's economic and financial power was affirmed. Outstanding evidence of this economic expansion was the coining in 1252 of the gold florin, which joined the silver florin coined as early as 1235. Symbol of the city (it was not by chance that the coin represented St. John the Baptist on one side and the Florentine lily on the other), the gold florin testified to the existence in 13th-century Florence of a flow of precious metal, furnished by commerce, which by this time was on a continental scale, and credit, which was to make the city the financial capital of the West.

During the period of the «Primo Popolo» the population of the city grew and new public buildings went up. In 1255 construction began on what was to be called the *Palazzo del Popolo*. The district of the Oltrarno was also furnished with stronger fortifications, utilizing for the scope material from the numerous towers which had been lopped off, and a fourth bridge, Santa Trinita, was built as already mentioned. The **Palazzo del Popolo** (now the **Bargello**) was erected to house the Councils of the Commune. With its imposing mass and its crenellated tower rising above all other city towers, it was the expression in architecture of the new political policy. The present aspect of the palace is the result of the integrations and additions of 1340-1345. Severe and suggestive, the unified massive block is lightly marked by the delicate cornice moldings which divide it into three stories, the second of which is softened by a succession of one and two-light openings.

The ill-omened day of the battle of Montaperti (1260) with the painful defeat of the Florentines by the Sienese hosts, determined the obliteration of all that the merchant middle class had accomplished politically. When the Ghibellines resumed power and restored the old institutions they decreed the destruction of the palaces and towers and houses which the principal exponents of the Guelph party owned in the city and in the surroundings. A valuable document of 1269, the *Liber Extimationum*, or *Book of the damage done*, tells us just how great the destruction inflicted by the Ghibelline party was. The city was covered with rubble, and 103 palaces, 580 houses and 85 towers were totally demolished not to speak of the partial damage done to other buildings. But despite this, incredible as it may seem, the economic development of the city does not seem to have suffered from all the damage inflicted on the architectural patrimony.

For six years Florence was forced to submit to the outrages of the great Ghibellines. It would have been destroyed had it not been for the fearless defense of Farinata degli Uberti at the convention of Empoli. But on the death of Manfredi (Feb. 26, 1266), the middle classes, defeated but not conquered, attempted to take over the government. The attempt failed, but the Ghibellines, fearing the power of the people, and deprived of imperial support, were forced to accept the services of Clement IV as peacemaker between the opposing factions. The pope openly favored the Guelph faction which thus succeeded in reconquering the power, with the aid of the knights of Charles of Anjou whose Italian expedition was financed by money from the Florentine bankers. Masters of the city, the Guelphs named Charles podestà for six years and reintroduced the political institutions abrogated by the Ghibellines.

In the meanwhile, notwithstanding a series of attempts (all of which failed) to make peace between the two factions, two new parties began to shape up among the people at large: the «Magnati» or entrepeneurs (persons whose aims were deemed dangerous to the populace as a whole, in other words the noble Guelphs and the repatriated Ghibellines, mostly large holders of houses and lands) and the «Popolani» or workers (merchant and artisans organized in guilds and in turn divided into «grassi» and «minuti» depending on the extent of their interests). Between 1282 and 1283 the *Arti Maggiori*, corresponding to the bourgeois business class, managed to introduce their own organs and institutions into the government. This was the beginning of the regime known as «Secondo Popolo» which was to lead to the constitution of the «Priorato» an institution which with all its ups and down was to represent the supremacy of the Guilds for almost two centuries. The new representatives of the Commune from then on were called «Priori delle Arti» (or later «Signori»). There were six of them, one for each civic quarter, with a «Difensore delle Arti e degli Artigiani, Capitano e Conservatore della pace del Comune di Firenze» at its head. The Magnati were not initially excluded from the government but in order to participate were obliged to join one of the Guilds. Later (1293), with the famous «Ordinamento di Giustizia» promoted by Giano della Bella, the historical process begun in the 12th century was to reach its natural conclusion - the Magnati were prohibited from taking part in the political life of the city. In the latter part of the 13th century Florence reached the zenith of its economic and demographic development. This was the period when great things were done in the fields of architecture and town planning, made possible by the formidable accumulations of capital that resulted from the expanding commercial and financial activities. The towered city, enclosed within a wall, was being replaced by an urban structure composed of a city «spread out in an equilibrium of open and built-up spaces» where «the urban landscape dominated by the recurring towers of the powerful private families was replaced by a landscape organized around large public structures» (G. Fanelli). The population which had continued to increase (according to Fiumi's figures there must have been more than 90,000 inhabitants) spread beyond the walls of 1172 creating new suburbs (*borghi*). New city *walls* were needed and in 1282 a belt

8,500 meters long was planned, with 73 tall towers and 15 gates equipped with their own towers, enclosing an area of 430 hectares, five times that of the precedent urban area. The size of the project based on an anticipated further expansion of the city (which was not to be), made it possible to include many fields and building areas together with the suburbs. The new city walls were planned so as to include within their circuit the extensions of the roads which departed from the gates of the precedent city wall. This explains the inclusion of the hills corresponding to Boboli and Costa San Giorgio. The Mugnone was naturally deviated once more and its waters, as before, filled the moats along the walls. These sixth (and last) city walls were the greatest financial commitment ever undertaken by the Florentine Commune. This was why work went on so slowly, interrupted more than once because of war and not finished until 1333. Much of the wall was demolished in the 19th century and only a few tracts, Oltrarno, and the principal gates, of which only one (Porta San Niccolò) has preserved its original height, are still extant. The ground plan of the walls however is still to be seen in the line of the avenues that run around the city periphery and for whose building they were demolished.

At the end of the 13th century Florence could rightly consider itself the main city of the West, as cited in the commemorative tablet of the construction of the church of *Santi Simone e Giuda* «... *de florentina (civitate) pre qualibet urbe latina...*» The entrepreneurs then in power decided to construct two great buildings which were in a sense to be symbols of the wealth and power of the city: the new cathedral and **Palazzo della Signoria**. Arnolfo di Cambio was the outstanding figure who designed both buildings, as well as all the other important works promoted by the government of the Guilds, including the new walls. The imposing palace-fortress for the residence of the Priors was begun in 1294 and its mass loomed over all other buildings in the city. Visualized as a great square block, topped by a projecting crenellated gallery, the building is characterized by the vigorous thrust of the high tower which surmounts it and which echoes three-dimensionally the terminating motif of the palazzo. The facing of rusticated ashlar in *pietra forte* accentuates its character of «keep and martial pride», and it is divided into three stories by cornice moldings on which the two-light windows circumscribed by round-headed arches rest.

In 1296 the reconstruction of the old cathedral of *Santa Reparata* was begun, a church which had become «... very coarse in its shape and small in comparison to a city of this kind». (G. Villani). The new building, no longer dedicated to the Palestinian saint, but to the Madonna, or more precisely **Santa Maria del Fiore**, was to undergo various changes in size and plan in the course of its construction which lasted for almost a century. Arnolfo's bold project was however basically maintained. The longitudinal scheme of a nave and two aisles was grafted onto a central plan building which fused the transept and the presbytery into a single organism and resulted in three tribunes in a trilobate arrangement around an enormous octagonal dome. The interior of the building is characterized by its great sense of space which dilates in all directions from the wide nave with its ogee cross vaulting springing from powerful composite piers (*multipli et uni*) connected to all the imposts of the arches. The

View of the Palazzo della Signoria by night.

The old fresco of the Stinche now in the Palazzo Vecchio, representing the Expulsion of the Duke of Athens.

replaced the tower houses with buildings in which the rooms were prevalently distributed horizontally, with the volumes relatively articulated and spread out and resulting in a greater complexity of layout. The massive cubes of the palaces with their regular facing of rusticated *pietra forte* were pierced by more and more openings, signs of a new, freer and less schematic concept of the organization and construction of space. The large **Palazzo Mozzi**, which dates to between 1260 and 1273, is one of the most conspicuous examples of the palaces that were built in this period. For decades it was considered the noblest civic building and it was not unusual for important personages in visit to the city to be lodged there. **Palazzo Ruggerini**, later Gianfigliazzi, between the Piazza Santa Trinita and the Santa Trinita bridge, is also of note, as well as the complex of **buildings** the Peruzzi erected around 1283 on the ruins of the Parlascio (the name the Florentines gave to the remains of the Roman amphitheater, a corruption of the Greek *perielaison* meaning circular space). Many other palaces of the late 13th century were later remodelled and now traces are still to be found in various architectural elements, (doors, windows, fragments of walls in sandstone blocks) in the buildings that line some of the oldest city streets such as Borgo San Jacopo, Borgo degli Albizi, Borgo Santi Apostoli, Via del Corso, Via Condotta, Via dei Cimatori, Via delle Terme, etc.

The austere facade of the Palazzo Mozzi.

construction of the great Franciscan church of *Santa Croce* is also attributed to Arnolfo di Cambio, as previously mentioned. Together with the Dominican *Santa Maria Novella* it represents another of the most prestigious monuments erected at the end of the 13th century under the government of the «Secondo Popolo».

When the city and the countryside were organized into districts (1292) and the building of the new city walls was begun, a whole new series of urban measures were undertaken with a view to opening new streets and widening or adapting the ones that were already there, so as to confer order, regularity, and decorum on the urban fabric which in the meanwhile was being enriched with new types of residential buildings. The numerous tower-houses (all of which have now been lopped off) were flanked by the palaces which the middle class merchants were building as a symbol and visible sign of their wealth and power. In the course of the 13th century, as we have seen, the tower-houses gradually modified their characteristics, with a greater number of openings that corresponded to the various rooms and, at times, an occasional decorative element (witness the **Amidei tower** with its two protruding lion protoma). The new 13th century type of tower-dwelling can be characterized by the fine **torre degli Alberti** in the Via dei Benci, the **torre dei Cerchi** in the street of the same name, the **torre dei Corbuzzi** in the Piazza San Pier Maggiore, the **torre dei Marsili**, in the Borgo san Jacopo, the **torre dei Foresi**, in the Via Porta Rossa the **torre dei Donati**, in the Borgo degli Albizi, to mention only a few of the better preserved ones.

But the new residences which the rich businessmen built from the late 13th century on were the fruit of a profound transformation of civil architecture which

THE HISTORICAL CENTER

PIAZZA DELLA SIGNORIA

The heart of civic life in ancient Florence. The **Neptune Fountain**, **Loggia dei Lanzi**, **Equestrian monument to Cosimo I de' Medici**.

LOGGIA DEI LANZI

Originally built to serve as the site for public ceremonies. It houses numerous Renaissance and antique works of sculpture.

PALAZZO VECCHIO

The residence of the Priors, a copy of Michelangelo's *David* is at the entrance. Inside: **Michelozzo's Courtyard**, the **Salone dei Cinquecento**, the **Studiolo of Francesco I**, the **State Apartments** and the collection of sculpture and paintings « **Works Refound** » (« **L'opera Ritrovata** »).

PALAZZO DEL BARGELLO (Via del Proconsolo)

Thirteenth-century headquarters for the Capitano del Popolo. Inside: the **Courtyard** and the **Museo Nazionale**.

MUSEO NAZIONALE DEL BARGELLO

The most important museum in the world for Renaissance sculpture. Inside: **Room of thirteenth-century sculpture**, the **Hall** with works by Michelangelo, Sansovino, Cellini, Giambologna and other artists. On the upper floors, the **Donatello Room**, the **Collections of Minor Arts**, the **Chapel of the Podestà**, the **Giovanni della Robbia Room**, the **Andrea della Robbia Room** and the **Verrocchio Room**.

PALAZZO DAVANZATI (Via Porta Rossa)

Typical Florentine palace. Inside: **Museum of the Florentine House**, with 16th-century furnishings. An idea of what a Renaissance house was like.

DUOMO

Cathedral designed by Arnolfo di Cambio over which Brunelleschi's great **Dome** looms. Inside: the precedent **Cathedral of S. Reparata** is in the subterranean chambers.

GIOTTO'S CAMPANILE

Fourteenth-century work designed by Giotto. The **terrace** at the top can be reached from the inside.

BAPTISTERY

Decorated outside by the three bronze doors; outstanding Ghiberti's **Gates of Paradise**. Inside: the *mosaics* which line the octagonal dome.

MUSEO DELL'OPERA DEL DUOMO (Piazza del Duomo)

Housing numerous works originally in S. Maria del Fiore and on Giotto's Campanile, including: Michelangelo's *Pictà*, the *choir-lofts by* Luca della Robbia and Donatello, and the *reliefs* from the Campanile as well as Donatello's *Magdalen*.

CHURCH OF ORSANMICHELE (Via Calzaioli)

On the lower floor of the large building which was formerly the grain market headquarters. Decorated on the exterior with numerous **tabernacles**. Inside, **Orcagna's Tabernacle**.

Above: general view of the Piazza della Signoria.
Facing page: the Neptune Fountain.

PIAZZA DELLA SIGNORIA

*One of the most scenographic squares in Italy was built
and enlarged between the 13th and 14th centuries, thanks
to the demolition of the palaces of the Uberti, Foraboschi
and other Ghibelline families. The asymmetrical complex
of the **Palazzo Vecchio**, on the northern side, dominates
the square. To the right is the **Loggia dei Lanzi**, a late
Gothic structure built by Benci di Cione and Simone
Talenti (1376-82), which houses a group of important
sculptures, including Cellini's famous Perseus and
Hercules and the Centaur by Giambologna. To the left of*
*the building is the lively **Neptune Fountain** by Bartolomeo
Ammannati and collaborators (1563-1575). Because of the
enormous white mass of the sea god set in the center of
the fountain on a chariot drawn by sea horses, the
Florentines renamed the sculpture « il Biancone », the
« White Giant », and the name has stuck. Particularly
interesting are the wonderful bronze figures at the base.
To one side stands the **Equestrian statue of Cosimo I**
(1594) by Giambologna. The square is surrounded by
interesting old palaces.*

LOGGIA DEI LANZI

The Loggia of the Signoria, known as the loggia of Orcagna (he supposedly designed it) or of the Lanzi (with reference to the mercenary guards of the Grand Duke Cosimo I), was built by Benci da Cione and Simone Talenti (1376-1391) for the public assemblies of the Signoria. The large round-headed arches are supported on compound piers, with accentuated horizontal rhythms. The airy elegance of the building is typically late Gothic. The fine relief panels above the piers depict allegorical figures of Virtues, executed between 1384 and 1389 on designs by Agnolo Gaddi. Two lions flank the entrance stairway: one is an example of classic art, the other is by Flaminio Vacca (1600). Various outstanding pieces of sculpture are sheltered in the loggia: on the left, Cellini's famous Perseus (1553); formerly on the right, the Rape of the Sabines by Giambologna of 1583 (now in the Galleria dell'Accademia); in the center, Hercules and the Centaur, also by Giambologna (1599); Ajax with the Body of Patrocles, a Hellenistic sculpture that has been reintegrated; and the Rape of Polyxena by Pio Fedi (1866). Six statues of matrons dating to Roman times are set against the back wall. A Latin inscription on the right wall, dating to 1750, refers to the substitution of the Florentine calendar (the beginning of the year on March 25th) with the normal calendar.

PERSEUS

This masterpiece in bronze by Benvenuto Cellini (1500-1571) is as splendid as it is famous. The artist signed the work on the strap that crosses the hero's chest in 1545-1554. Andromeda's liberator is shown just after he has cut off the Medusa's head. The features and the entire figure transmit the classic ideal of restrained force. The drama is over and the grave gesture (the hero's foot set on the monster's body) suggests achievement. According to tradition the complicated ornamentation of the winged helmet Perseus is wearing conceals a self-portrait of the artist. The bas-relief (a copy of the original now in the Bargello) with Perseus liberating Andromeda is in the pedestal where the refinement of execution and the decorative fantasy reveal Cellini's mastery as a goldsmith.

Facing page: views of the exterior and interior of the Loggia dei Lanzi. Right: Cellini's bronze Perseus.

COSIMO I DE' MEDICI
Grand Duke of Tuscany

The equestrian statue, situated in the center of the square, represents Cosimo I de' Medici and was made by Giambologna in 1594. The fiercely proud Florentine nobleman astride his powerful steed gives an impression of the utmost composure. The bas-reliefs of the pedestal celebrate the chief events in the life of the first Grand Duke of Tuscany: the Entry of Cosimo I in Siena, Pius V giving the grand-ducal insignia to Cosimo and the Tuscan Senate giving Cosimo the title of Duke of Florence. The statue is situated not far from the Palazzo Vecchio, where Cosimo I went to live in 1537, when he was eighteen, just after the death of Alessandro, murdered by Lorenzino de' Medici. Before him, the Medici family had ruled Florence for a long time, ever since they had taken part in the struggle between the Guilds and the common people, siding with the latter.

PALAZZO VECCHIO

Begun in 1294 and intended as a palace-fortress for the residence of the Priors, Arnolfo di Cambio conceived of the building as a large squared block terminated by a row of crenellations. It is characterized by the powerful thrust of the Tower of 1310 (94 m. high) which rises from the Gallery. Externally the structure is in rusticated ashlars of pietra forte which lend the large building, divided into three floors and decorated with two-light openings inscribed in round-headed arches, a highly impressive air and a sense of austerity. Between 1343 and 1592 modifications and additions were made to Arnolfo's original nucleus, both inside and out (Cronaca, Vasari, Buontalenti all worked on it). To be noted on the facade under the arches of the gallery are the frescoes with the nine coats of arms of the city communes. The mechanism of the clock dates to 1667. On either side the doorway are marble statues to hold chains, with above them an inscription Cosimo I had set there in 1551. Near the left hand corner of the palace is the Neptune Fountain by Ammannati.

Left: the equestrian statue of Cosimo I dei Medici. Facing page: the imposing mass of the Palazzo Vecchio.

Facing page, above: the entrance to Palazzo Vecchio with Hercules and Cacus; below, left: the courtyard by Michelozzo with Verrocchio's Putto and, to the right, the copy of Michelangelo's David.

Above: the interior of the asymmetrical Salone dei Cinquecento, richly decorated with painting and sculpture.

PALAZZO VECCHIO
FACADE
Various statues are lined up in front of the Palazzo Vecchio, including a copy of Michelangelo's David, that replaced the original in 1873, and the group of Hercules and Cacus by Bandinelli. On the facade, above the door, there is a medallion with the monogram of Christ between two lions in a blue field, surmounted by a gable. The inscription « Rex regum et Dominus dominantium » was placed there in 1551 by order of Cosimo I, to replace the previous inscription, set there thirty years before.

PALAZZO VECCHIO
INTERIOR
After passing through **Michelozzo's Court**, with gilded stucco columns and frescoes by Vasari, and with Verrocchio's Fountain with a Winged Putto holding a Fish in the center, Vasari's broad staircase leads to the imposing **Salone dei Cinquecento**, and to the **Studiolo of Francesco I**, created by Vasari and full of panels painted by Bronzino, Santi di Tito, Stradano, as well as bronze

statues by Giambologna and Ammannati. Access to the **State Apartments** is also from the Salone dei Cinquecento. The numerous rooms full of paintings and frescoes include the **Hall of Leo X** (at present occupied by the Mayor and the City Councilors); the **Hall of Clement VII** with Vasari's famous fresco of the Siege of Florence with a detailed view of the 16th-century city; the **Hall of Giovanni dalle Bande Nere**, the **Halls of Cosimo the Elder**, **Lorenzo the Magnificent** and of **Cosimo I**.

SALONE DEI CINQUECENTO
The Salone dei Cinquecento (prepared to house the assemblies of the Consiglio Generale del Popolo after the Medicis had been expelled from Florence for the second time) is by il Cronaca, while the frescoes were entrusted to Vasari. The allegorical paintings on the ceiling and the walls narrate the triumphal Return of Grand Duke Cosimo I to Florence, illustrate the possessions of the Medici Ducato and the Stories of the Conquest of Pisa and Siena. The marble statues include, on the right hand wall, Michelangelo's striking Genius of Victory.

Facing page, above, left: Michelangelo's Youth conquering Brute Force; right: Hercules and Diomedes by Vincenzo de' Rossi; below: Vasari's fresco of the Siege of Florence in the Hall of Clement VII.

Above, left: the coffered ceiling of the Salone dei Cinquecento; right: Francesco I's Studiolo. Below: Vasari's painting of Giovanni dei Medici coming to the aid of Ravenna, in the Hall of Leo X.

The original of the Putto with the fish, by Verrocchio.

The Green Room in the apartments of Eleonora of Toledo.

Below, left: the Priors' Chapel; right: Donatello's Judith.

SALA DEI GIGLI

*Of particular note among the State Apartments, after Vasari's **Apartment of Eleonora of Toledo** and the **Audience Hall**, is the **Sala dei Gigli**, which receives its name from the decorations of golden fleur de lis on a blue ground (ceiling by Giuliano da Maiano and Francione). The marble doorway that leads to the Audience hall is particularly fine. On the walls of the hall is a large fresco by Domenico Ghirlandaio.*

JUDITH: A RESTORED WORK OF ART

For centuries Donatello's masterpiece, Judith, which has recently been restored by the Opificio delle Pietre Dure (it took two years to complete the work), stood in the Piazza della Signoria. The bronze sculpture was removed from its original site in 1980 and transferred to the Audience Hall in Palazzo Vecchio. In 1986 it was once more moved so that it could be restored. Today the statue is once more there for the public to enjoy in all its splendid luminous forms inside the Palazzo in the large Sala dei Gigli where it can be perfectly preserved and protected from the elements.

Above: the interior of the Sala dei Gigli and, to the right, Donatello's Judith.

Facing page, above: the inlaid cabinet in the State Apartments; below: the room with the collections of « L'opera Ritrovata » (The Refound Work) dedicated to sculpture of the classical period.

Right: Leda and the Swan, attributed to the school of Leonardo da Vinci

THE COLLECTION
« L'OPERA RITROVATA »
This collection, installed in the rooms of Palazzo Vecchio, is the result of the commitment of Rodolfo Siviero, former minister for the recovery of stolen works of art, and of his long patient research. The exhibition, in fact, shows those works that during World War II were removed from Italy and dispersed in various countries. The exhibition is chronologically arranged: it starts with Roman sculpture and reliefs, goes on with numerous paintings among which there is a Leda with Swan, *originally attributed to Leonardo da Vinci, and works by Masaccio, Bronzino, Rubens and many others.*

Above: the Bargello with the tower of the Volognana which counterbalances the Campanile of the Badia. Below: a view from the Piazza S. Firenze. Facing page: two views of the Bargello courtyard with the loggia.

PALAZZO DEL BARGELLO

*The Palazzo del Bargello is like a fortress with powerful embattlements (the **Volognana**) surmounting the austere facade. It was built in 1255 as the seat of the Capitano del Popolo, and the Podestà and the Consiglio di Giustizia were then housed there. In 1574 it became the living quarters for the Bargello (Captain of Justice, or chief of police). The exterior, articulated by cornices, has lintelled windows in the lower part and two-light openings or simple windows further up. The crenellation at the top juts out supported on small arches and corbels. The interior is centered around a **courtyard** with porticoes on three sides, with piers and arcading. A picturesque **covered staircase**, built in the l4th century by Neri di Fioravante, leads to the upper **loggia**, by Tone di Giovanni (1319). The walls of the courtyard are covered with dozens of coats of arms of the various Podestà and Giudici di Ruota. Since 1859 the place has been the site of the **Museo Nazionale** (one of the most important in the world) which contains Renaissance sculpture and masterpieces of the minor arts from varying periods.*

Above: the hall on the lower floor of the Bargello with the collection of Renaissance sculpture. Left: the bust of Cosimo I by Cellini. Facing page, above: Leda and the Swan by Ammannati; below, left: a marble bust of Cosimo I by Baccio Bandinelli, and, to the right, Michelangelo's Brutus.

MUSEO NAZIONALE DEL BARGELLO

*The enormous **Entrance hall** on piers with solid vaulting has heraldic decorations on the walls with the coats of arms of the podestà (13th-14th cent.).*
*From here to the scenographic **Courtyard** which is irregular and unique. The coats of arms of many podestà are here and, under the portico, the picturesque insignia of the quarters and the districts into which the city was once divided. Various 16th-century statues set against the walls are by Bandinelli, Ammannati, Giambologna and Danti.*
*The courtyard leads to a **Hall** with a collection of 14th-century sculpture, including Tino da Camaino's Madonna and Child with Angel, a meditating Madonna and Child of Venetian school, the base of a holy water stoup by Nicola Pisano and a Madonna between St. Peter and St. Paul by Paolo di Giovanni (circa 1328). In the Room close to the open staircase are important works by Michelangelo: the Bacchus (1470), an early work of great power despite the softness of form, the Pitti Tondo, with the Madonna teaching Jesus and St. John to read (1504), the David or Apollo (1530), the Brutus (1540). There are also works by Ammannati, Giambologna (including his famous Mercury of 1564) Tribolo, Danti, Francavilla and Sansovino who made a Bacchus of his own to compete with Michelangelo's. The bronze bust of Cosimo I by Cellini, made for Portoferraio in Elba and brought back in 1781, is also in the same room.*

40

41

Above, left: the Pitti Tondo by Michelangelo; right: the bust of Michelangelo by Daniele da Volterra. Facing page, above left: Bacchus by Sansovino, done in competition with Michelangelo's Bacchus (on the right). Below, left: the model for Cellini's Perseus, and, on the right, Giambologna's Mercury.

The Open Staircase, *leads to the* **Loggia**, *ornamented with various works by other 16th-century artists.*
The first room to the right, once the Salone del Consiglio Generale, is now the **Donatello Room** *and contains many of his works such as the* St. George *(1416) with its self-contained energy, made for the niche in Orsanmichele, the young* St. John, *slender and mystical, the marble* David *(1408) and the bronze* David, *the first delicate Renaissance nude made around 1430. Also by Donatello are the* Marzocco, *the symbol of the city, and the lively bronze* Amor-Attis, *revealing a classic influence. In addition to works by Luca della Robbia, Ghiberti, Vecchietta and Agostino di Duccio, the room also contains the trial panels which Ghiberti and Brunelleschi made in 1402 for the competition (there were six contestants) for the second doors of the Florentine Baptistery. Ghiberti's relief succeeds in giving us an organically complete vision of the story of the* Sacrifice of Isaac *while Brunelleschi's panel, well articulated as it is, gives the impression of a juxtaposition of parts.*
Access to the **Collection of Decorative Arts,** *mostly based on the donation of the Carrand Collections, is from the hall. Goldwork and enamels from the Middle Ages to the 16th century, seals and various metal objects are in the* **Salone del Podestà.**
In the adjacent **Cappella del Podestà,** *where those condemned to death passed their last hours, there are*

Above: the interior of the upper Loggia of the Bargello; below: the Madonna of the Rose Garden, by Luca della Robbia. Facing page, above: the Donatello Room and, below: a lunette by Luca della Robbia with the Madonna and Child with Angels.

Giottesque frescoes with Paradise, Hell and Stories of the Saints. *The floor is completed by the* **Sala degli Avori**, *with rare carvings from the ancient period to the 15th century; the* **Sala delle Oreficerie**, *with numerous works of sacred art, and the* **Sala delle Majoliche**.
The second floor of the Bargello contains other rooms dedicated to great artists: the first, known as the **Giovanni della Robbia Room**, *contains a number of the master's sculptures including the predella with Christ and Saints, St. Dominic, the Pietà and the Annunciation.*
The following **Andrea della Robbia Room** *houses the* Madonna degli Architetti *and other works in glazed terracotta. In the* **Verrocchio Room** *are the* Resurrection, *the* bust of a young woman, *the* Madonna and Child, *the* bronze David *and other works by the master as well as various* busts *and sculpture by Mino da Fiesole and the group of* Hercules and Antaeus *by Pollaiolo, with the vibrating force of the two struggling figures. Other bronze sculpture is in the* **Sala dei Bronzetti** *with the* mantelpiece of Casa Borgherini *by Benedetto da Rovezzano; the* **Sala delle Armi** *houses military paraphernalia from the Middle Ages to the 17th century. The museum is completed by the* **Sala della Torre** *with tapestries and the* **Medagliere Mediceo** *with works by artists such as Pisanello, Cellini, Michelozzo and others.*

45

Facing page, left: Donatello's bronze David, and, on the right, his marble David.

Above, left: the bust of Niccolò da Uzzano and, on the right, the Marzocco, both by Donatello. Below: the two panels prepared for the competition for the second doors of the Baptistery: on the left the one by Brunelleschi, on the right the one by Ghiberti.

Above: the Chapel of the Podestà with frescoes by Giotto. To the side, a detail of the fresco on the back wall with the portrait of Dante Alighieri (at the center of the picture).

PALAZZO DAVANZATI

Built around 1330, externally the base is in rusticated pietra forte ashlars. The upper floors display a smoother facade which contains typically Florentine windows with a round-headed arch in the intrados. On the top of the building is the 15th-century terrace covered with a gabled watershed. On the right the typical « chiassolo » should be noted. The palace (which belonged to the Davizzi family in the 14th century, and then in the second half of the 16th century to the Davanzatis who restored it) is a superb example of the 14th-century upper-class dwelling. Today it houses the **Museo della Casa Fiorentina**, an interesting collection of furniture and household objects from the 15th and 16th centuries.

Right: the picturesque courtyard of the Palazzo Davanzati. Below: one of the rooms with frescoes, period furnishings, part of the Museo della Casa Fiorentina.

THE CATHEDRAL

DUOMO

Dedicated to S. Maria del Fiore, the Cathedral is the fruit of the dedicated work of the many artists who collaborated in its building for various centuries. In 1294 the Corporation of the Guilds commissioned Arnolfo di Cambio with the realization of a new Cathedral that was to replace the extant church of Santa Reparata. The cathedral workshop grew up around and inside the church, which continued to be used for decades, until 1375. Work on the new Cathedral or Duomo began on Sept. 8, 1296 and continued under various capomastri or directors of works such as Giotto, Andrea Pisano, Francesco Talenti, until 1375, when Santa Reparata was torn down and part of Arnolfo's project was altered. The **dome** had to wait until 1420, the year in which Brunelleschi won the competition for the building of this enormous structure. In 1434 work was terminated and two years later the church was consecrated, 140 years after it had been begun. The **lantern** was started in 1445 and finished in 1461 with the gilded sphere. The facade is in 19th-century Gothic style.

DOME

Brunelleschi's masterpiece, planned and raised between 1420 and 1434, put the finishing touch on the building of the Duomo. The great artist proposed to build the enormous airy dome without the use of fixed centering, thanks to the employment of ribbing with tie beams and bricks set in herringbone patterns, a double shell for the dome with an ogive form (at the drum the dome is 45.52 m. in diameter and 91 m. high) on a tall drum. The interior of the dome, which Brunelleschi envisioned bare, was frescoed by Vasari and Zuccari (1572-1579). In the 19th century, and recently, proposals have been made to restore the dome to its original pristine whiteness. The **lantern** was also designed by Brunelleschi and is in the form of a temple, raising the total height of the church to 107 meters.

Facing page and above: the Duomo and Brunelleschi's dome.

Left: the Campanile designed and partly built by Giotto. Facing page: the neogothic facade of the Cathedral.

GIOTTO'S CAMPANILE

The Cathedral bell tower was begun in 1334 by Giotto, who as capomastro was overseer for the construction of the Duomo.

Up to his death in 1337, he built the bottom part of the campanile comprised of two closed stages decorated with hexagonal and rhomboid reliefs, by Andrea Pisano, Luca della Robbia, Alberto Arnoldi and workshop. The relief panels on the lower band, now replaced by casts, represent the Life of Man with Genesis and Arts and Industries executed by Andrea Pisano and Luca della Robbia to Giotto's designs.

The two upper stages were carried to completion by Andrea Pisano, who took Giotto's place at the time. He created a series of sixteen niches between the pilaster strips which contained statues of the Prophets, Sibyls and the Baptist, surmounted by an equal number of false niches. Between 1350 and 1359 Francesco Talenti finished the campanile, adding two levels with the two gabled two-light windows with their lovely twisted columns and the stage with the single three-light opening.

DUOMO
FACADE

Arnolfo di Cambio's unfinished facade of the Duomo was torn down in 1587. From then on, for almost three centuries, there was a continuous flow of projects and competitions for the new facade of the Cathedral until finally in 1871 the design presented by the architect Emilio de Fabris was approved (work ended in 1887). The facade betrays the historical point of view which ruled the taste of the times and employed the same types of marble previously used in the rest of the building - Carrara white, Prato green and Maremma pink. Above the three portals with Stories of Mary are three lunettes with, from left to right, Charity, the Madonna with the Patron Saints of the City, and Faith; the pediment over the central portal has a Madonna in Glory. The statues of the Apostles and of Mary are set in the frieze that runs between the rose windows at the sides and the one in the center. Above, after a series of busts of artists, is the pediment with the low relief of God the Father.

Above: the interior of the Duomo of Florence. Below: the bust of Filippo Brunelleschi. Facing page, above: the panel by Domenico di Michelino with Dante and the Divine Comedy; below, left: equestrian monument to Niccolo da Tolentino, fresco by Andrea del Castagno, and, on the right, Paolo Uccello's Monument to John Hawkwood (Giovanni Acuto), fresco.

DUOMO
INTERIOR

*In line with the dictates of Italian Gothic architecture there is a strong feeling for vertical and horizontal space inside the Duomo (the fourth largest church in the world: 153 meters long, 38 meters wide across the nave and aisles, and 90 at the transept). In the nave and aisles, piers with pilaster strips support large moderately pointed arches and ribbed Gothic vaulting. A gallery on corbels runs along on high. At the back is the high altar (by Baccio Bandinelli) surrounded by three apses or **tribunes**, each subdivided into five rooms. The polychrome marble pavement (1526-1660) is by Baccio and Giuliano d'Agnolo, Francesco da Sangallo and others. The two equestrian monuments (frescoes transferred from the wall) of John Hawkwood (Giovanni Acuto) and Niccolò da Tolentino are on the wall of the left aisle. The former, of 1436, is by Paolo Uccello; the latter, of 1456, by Andrea del Castagno (note the diversity in the modelling of the figures of these two mercenary captains: severity as opposed to vitality). To be noted among the many other works are the Tomb of Antonio d'Orso by Tino di Camaino (1321); the lunette with the Crowned Madonna by Gaddo Gaddi; and in the left aisle the tabernacle with Joshua by Ciuffagni, Donatello and Nanni di Bartolo; the Bust of Squarcialupi by da Maiano, the panels with Saints Cosmas and Damian by Bicci di Lorenzo.*

QVI COELVM CECINIT MEDIVMQVE IMVMQVE TRIBVNAL · LVSTRAVITQVE ANIMO CVNCTA POETA SVO · DOCTVS ADEST DANTES SVA QVEM FLORENTIA SAEPE
SENSIT CONSILIIS AC PIETATE PATREM · NIL POTVIT TANTO MORS SAEVA NOCERE POETAE · QVEM VIVVM VIRTVS CARMEN IMAGO FACIT

Above: a stretch of the walls of the old Cathedral of S. Reparata in the subterraneans of the Duomo. Facing page, above: the tomb of Filippo Brunelleschi, and, below: fragments of a fresco with the Passion of Christ.

SANTA REPARATA
The old cathedral of Florence was originally built in the 4th-5th centuries on the ruins of a Roman domus, with columns dividing the nave from the two side aisles and a single apse. During the Byzantine wars the church was destroyed, to be rebuilt between the 7th and 9th centuries. The perimeter remained almost the same but the building was enriched by two side chapels and the columns were replaced by piers with engaged pilasters. Between the year 1000 and 1100 a crypt was added under the apse and the choir was raised, while two bell towers were built near the apse. When the new Cathedral of Santa Maria del Fiore was built, this ancient church, dedicated to the young saint who died a martyr in Caesarea, had to relinquish its site. The new Cathedral however was built around the old church which was not torn down until its completion in 1375. In 1966 when the pavement of the Duomo had to be restored, remains of the preceding cathedral came to light. Now an entrance situated between the first and second piers of the right aisle of the Duomo leads down into a spacious chamber where, thanks to the structures installed by the architect Morozzi, the remains of frescoes which once decorated the church, the tombstones of various prelates and civil authorities (as well as the slab which indicates Brunelleschi's tomb), and stretches of the brick and mosaic pavements can still be seen.

BAPTISTERY

This octagonal building with semicircular apses, raised on a stepped podium, was originally built in the 4th-5th centuries near the north gate of Roman Florence. Its current appearance dates to the 11th-13th centuries: the smooth pyramidal roof was terminated in 1128, the **lantern** with columns dates to 1150, the rectangular **tribune** (the « scarsella ») to 1202. The exterior is faced with green and white marble. Each side is divided into three sections by pilaster strips surmounted by trabeation and round arches with windows. Particularly striking are the bronze doors and, inside, the mosaics in the dome.

BAPTISTERY
GATES OF PARADISE

There are three sets of doors in the Baptistery of San Giovanni: the **south doors** by Andrea Pisano with Stories of the life of the Baptist and Allegories of the Virtues, the **north doors** by Ghiberti, with Stories from the New Testament, Evangelists and Doctors of the Church, and the **east doors** (or Gates of Paradise), Ghiberti's masterpiece and deservedly the most famous of the three. They are divided into ten panels which depict Stories from the Old Testament and were commissioned by the Arte dei Mercanti in 1425. In the perfection of execution, they are worthy of the name Michelangelo bestowed on them. Small figures of biblical personages and portraits of contemporary artists are to be found in the frame around the panels.

Facing page and on this page: various views of the Baptistery of S. Giovanni.

**GATES OF PARADISE:
EPISODES FROM THE OLD
TESTAMENT DEPICTED IN THE TEN
PANELS.**

Creation of Adam and Eve. The Fall. The Expulsion from Paradise.	Work of the first men. Sacrifice of Cain and Abel. Cain kills Abel. God reproves Cain.
Noah and his family offering sacrifice after having left the ark. Drunkenness of Noah.	The Angels appear to Abraham. Sacrifice of Isaac.
Birth of Esau and Jacob. Sale of the birthright of the first-born. Isaac orders Esau to go hunting. Esau out hunting. Rebekah counsels Jacob. Isaac is deceived.	Joseph sold to the merchants. Discovery of the cup of gold in Benjamin's sack. Joseph reveals himself to his brothers.
On Mount Sinai Moses receives the Tables of the Law.	The people of Israel in the River Jordan. The Fall of Jericho.
Battle against the Philistines. David kills Goliath.	Solomon receives the Queen of Sheba.

**BAPTISTERY
GATES OF PARADISE**

The Gates of Paradise are currently being restored and a perfect copy has been set in their place. The photos published were taken of the originals and show the panels in their original splendor before atmospheric agents and pollution covered them with a black patina. The doors there now are bright and shiny and this is probably what they looked like when first placed in the Baptistery in 1425. Eventually they too will be covered by a patina while the restored originals will remain safely sheltered in the Museo dell'Opera del Duomo.

Details of the heads of Lorenzo Ghiberti and his son Vittorio.

Drunkenness of Noah.

Creation ot Adam.

Cain killing Abel.

Isaac orders Esau to go hunting.   Discovery of the gold cup.   Sibyl and a biblical personage.

BAPTISTERY
INTERIOR

The interior of the Baptistery is characterized by the walls on two orders, the inferior one with columns and the upper one with pillars between mullioned windows. The surfaces are covered by marble geometrical tarsias, similar to those of the floor. Particularly interesting the tomb of the Antipope John XXIII, a complex built by Michelozzo and Donatello (the latter made the reclining statue), two Roman sarcofagi and the tomb slab of Bishop Ranieri. The **apse** is enriched by beautiful mosaics of the thirteenth century, coeval to those of the large dome. Next to the large Enthroned Christ by Coppo di Marcovaldo, six tiers of bands representing, from the base to the top, scenes from the life of Saint John the Baptist, stories of Christ, of Joseph, of Genesis, Celestial Hierarchies and ornamental motifs.

Facing page: the South Doors of the Baptistery, by Andrea Pisano, with the Stories of the Baptist. This page, above: interior of the Baptistery, and, to the right, the Tomb of the Anti-Pope John XXIII designed by Michelozzo and Donatello.

Following two pages. Left: a view of the interior of the cupola of the Baptistery with the arch of the *scarsella* and its mosaics. Right: the octagon of the cupola completely lined with mosaic decoration.

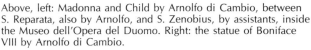

Above, left: Madonna and Child by Arnolfo di Cambio, between S. Reparata, also by Arnolfo, and S. Zenobius, by assistants, inside the Museo dell'Opera del Duomo. Right: the statue of Boniface VIII by Arnolfo di Cambio.

Facing page, above: Donatello's choir-loft; below: Donatello's Magdalen between two prophets originally on Giotto's Campanile; the one on the left, Habacuc, has been nicknamed « Lo Zuccone » (Pumpkin head).

MUSEO DELL'OPERA DEL DUOMO

The museum is situated across from the apse of the Cathedral and contains works of art from the Duomo, the Campanile and the Baptistery. Over the entrance is the Bust of Cosimo I by Bandini. Inside are Romanesque sculpture, statues and remains of the original facade of the Duomo and the Baptistery. Works on the ground floor include the statues of the Blessing Boniface VIII, Arnolfo di Cambio's Madonna and Child and his Madonna of the Nativity, as well as Nanni di Banco's famous St. Luke. In an adjacent room books, illuminated chorales and reliquaries. On the first floor is the room with the choir-loft, by Luca della Robbia (1431-1438) with ten reliefs inspired by the joyous Psalm of King David, and Donatello's choir-loft (1433-1439), with a severe architectural layout inspired by classical antiquity. These two masterpieces in marble were removed from the Duomo in 1686 by Ferdinando de' Medici. The same room contains the statues which once stood on the Campanile, such as Donatello's figures of the prophets Habacuc, known as lo Zuccone (Pumpkin head), and Jeremiah, and Nanni di Bartolo's Abraham and Isaac. In the room to the left are to be found the original panels from Giotto's campanile, arranged in their original order. Outstanding examples by Andrea Pisano in the lower tier include the famous Creation of Adam, Creation of Eve and Working of the Land; those in the upper tier are by the

school of Pisano and by Alberto Arnoldi and depict the Sacraments. In the room to the right is the lovely altar frontal from the Baptistery, a magnificent example of Gothic goldwork with gilding and enamel, which was not completed until the Renaissance. Michelozzo, Verrocchio, Antonio del Pollaiolo and Bernardo Cennini all collaborated on this masterpieces.

On either side are statues of the Virgin of the Annunciation and the Archangel Gabriel, attributed to Jacopo della Quercia. Other examples of painting and sculpture which draw our attention in the museum, apart from Michelangelo's famous Deposition, include a noteworthy diptych with Stories of Christ and the Madonna, late 13th-century Byzantine school, and above all, halfway down the stairs, the Magdalen, an intense wooden statue by Donatello. The almost feverish execution and the material itself make this pathetically moving work seem real. The figure belongs to Donatello's last Florentine period (to be dated between 1435 and 1455) and recent restoration has restored it to its original coloring. Back on the ground floor it is of interest to study the drawing dating to the second half of the 16th century which depicts the original facade of the Duomo, before it was torn down in 1587, and the placing of the statues and architectonic decorations, many of which were salvaged and are on display in this same room.

On the two pages: the original panels from Luca della Robbia's choir-loft, now inside the Museo dell'Opera del Duomo.

MUSEUM DELL'OPERA DEL DUOMO
CHOIR-LOFTS BY LUCA DELLA ROBBIA AND DONATELLO
The two 15th-century choir-lofts, originally placed in the Cathedral under the dome, give the room its name. The **choir-loft by Donatello**, carried out between 1433 and 1439, consists of a large balustrade supported by five consoles. A continuous frieze of dancing putti (winged children) moves riotously behind a kind of open gallery with pairs of columns. The frieze as well as the abundant ornamentation of the balustrade and the lower part hark back to the classical art of the Late Roman period, studied by Donatello during his stay in Rome.
Quite different is the **choir-loft by Luca della Robbia**, a reconstruction

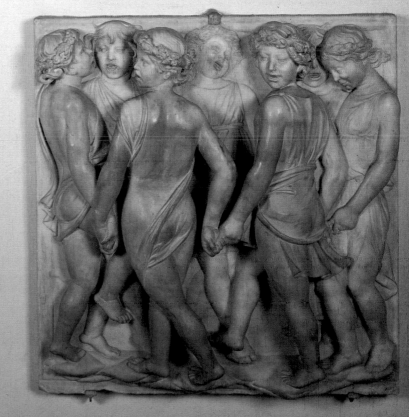

using the original architectonic parts
and casts of the ten panels. The
originals are at the entrance of the
room. Even though the structural
design is similar, the choir-loft by
Luca della Robbia is the result of a
different interpretation of the Roman
spirit and draws its inspiration from
the art of the early Empire. The front
of the cantoria is more massive and
less airy than Donatello's, the panels
with figures of dance, song and
music in relief are scanned by pairs
of grooved pilasters. Other similar
panels are placed at either end. The
scenes illustrate the 150th Psalm
from King David, which is inscribed
in its entirety. Like Donatello's, this
choir-loft was removed from the
Cathedral in 1686, when more space
was required on the occasion of the
wedding of Ferdinando de' Medici.

MICHELANGELO'S PIETÀ
This sculpture was originally in the Duomo. The central figure has been interpreted as a self-portrait of the artist. The Pietà was sculptured between 1550 and 1553 by Michelangelo for his chapel in S. Maria Maggiore in Rome. It remained, however, in the underground storerooms of S. Lorenzo until 1722 when it was transferred to the Duomo. It is probably one of Michelangelo's most dramatic pieces, an example of his painterly use of rough shaping (his famous « non-finito »). The restoration of Christ's left arm and the figure of the Magdalen were carried out by his pupil Tiberio Calcagni.

Left: wooden model of a project for the facade of the Duomo. Below, left: various hexagonal and rhomboid panels from Giotto's bell tower. Facing page: Michelangelo's Pietà.

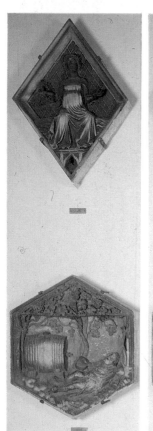

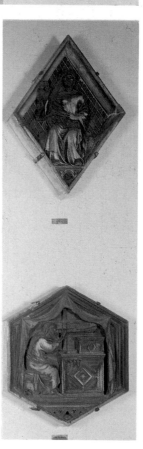

CHURCH OF ORSANMICHELE

Once a loggia used as a grain market (built by Arnolfo di Cambio, 1290), it was destroyed in a fire in 1304. Rebuilt in 1337 (the work of Francesco Talenti, Neri di Fioravante and Neri di Cione), between 1380 and 1404 the structure was transformed into a church. The austere lines of the large cubic building (with the arcading serving as a base) are softened by the late Gothic marble decoration. The upper part is in pietra forte with two tiers of large two-light openings. Niches and tabernacles with statues are set into the outer walls (particularly famous are Ghiberti's St. John the Baptist, 1414-16; Verrocchio's St. Thomas, 1464-83; Nanni di Banco's Four Crowned Martyrs, 1408; the copy of Donatello's St. George, 1416). Inside the church is the imposing Tabernacle by Orcagna, in flamboyant Gothic style (1355-59).

Facing page: the square building with the Church of Orsanmichele on the ground floor. This page, right: Orcagna's Tabernacle and, below, the interior of the church.

FROM THE FOURTEENTH CENTURY TO THE RENAISSANCE

Towards the end of the 13th century and in the early 14th century the contrasts between the *popolo minuto* (middle and lower middle classes) and the *popolo grasso* (wealthy merchants) were accentuated. The latter had a firm grip on the power, since the Priors were chosen exclusively from representatives of the Arti maggiori, who also held the majority in the Councils of the Republic. In the 14th century the *popolo minuto* tried several times to broaden the democratic base of the government by increasing the participation of the Arti minori in the government. In 1378, under the impulse of a movement set in motion by the proletariat led by a wool-carder, Michele de Lando, the *popolo grasso* were obliged to accept an institutional reform which not only extended the right to elect one of their representatives as Prior to all the guilds but also provided for the constitution of three new Guilds (Tintori, Farsettai, Dyers, Corseteers and Ciompi: the revolt was to take its name from latter) corresponding to the most humble activities and the workers. But due to internal divergent interests and an incapacity to govern, the *popolo minuto* was unable to withstand the reaction of the large merchant middle classes which soon once more took over power.

The rivalry between the Donati family which had become noble and the Cerchi family resulted in much dissension and led to the formation of two antagonistic groups of political factions to be known as *Neri* and *Bianchi* or Blacks and Whites. The former were generally exponents of the «*gente nova dai subiti guadagni*» (newcomers with easy profits) such as the Cerchi, who had recently come from the country and had quickly made a fortune. The Neri, under the guidance of Corso Donati grouped together the representatives of the old noble classes and the most intransigent Guelphists. The two parties took turns at the priorate in the last decade of the 13th century but from then on the conflict was intensified. The Priors were forced to exile the heads of the two factions, and the situation precipitated. The Neri invoked the intervention of the pope who sent as his peacemaker Charles of Valois, the brother of Philip Le Belle, king of France.

He openly favored the Neri, and even had the heads of the Bianchi arrested and forced those who were most compromised, including Dante Alighieri, into exile.

In addition to these internal struggles, the city had also to sustain the onerous burden of the wars against the powerful Ghibelline signorias of the Visconti and the Scaligeri, joined by the Pisans and the Luccans. The «foreign» policies of the merchant classes were aimed at maintaining the Guelph alliance which reunited «a military force, an economic power and a spiritual and moral power that all complemented each other per-

fectly» (Y. Renouard). Two serious defeats (Montecatini, August 29, 1315 and Altopascio, Sept. 23, 1325) induced Florence first to ask for the protection of the Angevin troops (accompanied by the government of a viceroy of King Robert's), then to place themselves under the direct dominion of the house of Anjou, in the person of Charles, duke of Calabria. The death of the duke in 1327 unexpectedly restored its freedom to the Florentine Commune. But it did not end there. A new attempt to take over Pisa and Lucca failed miserably. The Florentines, defeated by the Ghibelline forces under the leadership of the lord of Verona, Martino della Scala (1339), were once more forced to ask King Robert for aid. This resulted in a brief tyranny by a viceroy of the king, Gualtierio di Brienne, duke of Athens, who even succeeded in getting himself nominated lord for life. The tyranny ended on July 26, 1343, on the day of Saint Anne, and the people, tired of violence and abuses of power, threw out the tyrant and restored the civic liberties.

During the 14th century, internal strife and wars were aggravated by famine and epidemics (particularly deadly the plague of 1348) which made a situation that was already precarious even more grievous. It was a period of decisive juncture common to all Western economy. Further damage was caused by the disastrous flood of 1333 which also swept away all the bridges over the Arno except the Rubaconte. The 14th century was therefore a century of political and economic crisis, apart from the fact that epidemics reduced the population by half. The crisis was also reflected in the city's architectural activity which continued at a much slower pace than before. The buildings that saw the light in the 14th century, even if on the whole greatly inferior to those of the preceding century, were nonetheless outstanding achievements and the expression of a precise cultural will on the part of a ruling class which disposed of a productive structure with a noteworthy capacity for the accumulation of capital. From the point of view of town planning the city settled into the form already established by the developments of the 13th century. Building activity turned first of all to finishing the great undertakings of the end of the 13th century (the *walls*, the *cathedral*, the *Palazzo della Signoria*, the large monastic complex) and to reconstructing the bridges which had been destroyed. The first of these to be rebuilt, between 1334 and 1337, was the Ponte alla Carraia, apparently after a design by Giotto. The reconstructions of the other bridges, from the **Ponte Vecchio** on, were based on this bridge. The *Ponte Vecchio* was built by Taddeo Gaddi in three sweeping arches with a road much wider than before. Particular care was paid to the reconstruction of the shops (which were originally in wood) and which were

The Loggia del Bigallo on the corner between Piazza del Duomo and Via Calzaioli.

arranged at either side in low crenellated buildings open at the base with wide arches. A free space was however left at the center of the bridge so that «there would be a sweeping view up and down the river, towards the banks and towards the lovely hills around» (G. Dati). At the beginning of the 16th century the shops became private property and were modified in height and size. The symmetry of the whole gave way to the picturesqueness we know now.

Other public buildings were enlarged or rebuilt (the *Palazzo del Podestà*, for example, and the *Palazzo della Signoria* itself) and new structures went up as the city's social fabric changed. To one side of the Cathedral, where work for the new church was intermittently being carried out (*Santa Reparata* within the Cathedral workyards continued to be used for worship until it was demolished in 1375), the Gothic **Loggia del Bigallo** (1352-1358) was built and **Giotto's tower** (1334-1359) was raised to a height of 80 meters. Until the construction of Brunelleschi's dome, the campanile and the tower of the *Palazzo della Signoria* were the two principal landmarks of the city. In centuries past the towers had served as the emblems for the major political factions and now two vertical elements (the tower of the *Palazzo della Signoria* and *Giotto's bell tower*) became symbols of the power of the city taken as a whole. Elegant and slender but at the same time powerful and with angular projections emphasizing its solidity, the campanile was begun by Giotto in 1334, continued by Andrea Pisano and finished by Francesco Talenti between 1348 and 1359. The tower is divided into five

stages (Giotto's part goes as far as the second stage) and is animated by a facing of geometric designs in polychrome marble and by superposed windows which gradually lighten the mass of the tower from bottom to top. At the base is a decoration of panels with bas-reliefs representing the activities of man, surmounted by a row of niches containing statues of the prophets and the sibyls. The greatest exponents of Tuscan sculpture of the 14th and 15th centuries had a hand in the decoration and included Andrea da Pontedera, Nanni di Bartolo, Luca della Robbia, Donatello.

In turn the *Palazzo della Signoria* was completed with the monumental **Loggia dei Lanzi** for public ceremonies, the work of Benci di Cione and Simone Talenti (1376-391). With its large round arches on polystyle piers and its accentuated horizontal rhythms, the imposing structure seems a prelude to Renaissance architecture. The same sense of space is to be met with in the nearby **Orsanmichele**, built from 1337 on by Francesco Talenti, Neri di Fioravante and Benci di Cione. Created as a loggia-market for wheat and oats, the building was transformed into an oratory as early as 1357, even while the large storerooms for grain were being added on top. The resulting building was an enormous paralleliped with the arches of the Loggia at the base, filled in with a late Gothic marble decoration, flamboyant and delicate, that contrast with the upper part and its uniform walls in *pietra forte* lightened by two orders of wide two-light windows with slightly pointed arches. Tabernacles containing statues of the patron saints of the Guilds were later to be set in the pilasters between the arches. The statues were produced from the middle of the 14th century up through the entire 16th century and include some of the major works of Renaissance sculpture, such as Donatello's *St. George* (*tabernacle of the Armaioli or armourers*), Ghiberti's *St. Matthew* (*tabernacle of the Cambio or bankers*), Verrocchio's *Doubting Thomas* (*tabernacle of the Mercanzia or merchant's tribunal*), Nanni di Banco's *St. Eligius* (*tabernacle of the Maniscalchi or smiths*).

Florentine 14th-century architecture continued to produce great spatial structures, soberly decorated, with a geometric clarity of pattern, stressed by the clear-cut three dimensionality of the structural arrangement. The minor buildings also displayed the same features and included the limited number of churches renovated in the 14th century: **San Niccolò sopr'Arno**, whose bare interior with a single nave was covered with the traditional open timber roof; **San Remigio**, divided into a nave and two aisles by a system of octagonal piers from which the ogee vaulting sprang; **San Carlo de' Lombardi**, a simple little church built across from Orsanmichele from 1349 on and formerly dedicated to Saint Anne and then to St. Michael; **San Giovannino dei Cavalieri**, also with a nave and two aisles, simply covered by a wooden truss roof.

After the impressive expansion of the 13th century, the city began to take shape and what might be called a real town planning policy attempted to provide the inchoate building fabric with some degree of order and regularity. Throughout the 14th century one provision after another was taken in an effort to broaden the streets or modify their routes; to tear down ramshackle buildings or those with superstructures (such as projections or external stairs) which impeded traffic. The main scope of the Commune's town planning policy (widen and straighten the streets) was on the whole successfully accomplished in the sector that lay between the last two city walls, but was much more difficult in the older heart of the city. Public intervention, at least in most cases, was based on considerations of «decorum». «For the greater beauty of the city» new piazzas were created or renovated; it was decreed that the houses were to have a stone facing on their lower part, certain activities were prohibited because they were antihygienic; unhealthy areas were to be reclaimed. Naturally the Commune's first obligations were in the reorganization of the city's two principal piazzas (Piazza della Signoria and the area around the complex of *Cathedral and Baptistery*, which required the demolition of various structures) as well as the broadening of the Via de' Calzaioli to unite the two piazzas. As can often still be seen, the buildings that line this street have a facade with rough-hewn blocks of *pietra forte* at least in the bottom part, and a series of regular arches in correspondence to the ground floor, features that had already appeared in some of the buildings in the Piazza della Signoria and in those set behind the apse of the *Duomo*. Loggias and large arcades were frequently used in civil architecture of the 14th century where the ground-floor rooms served as warehouses or shops and the vaulted loggias were reserved for the official family ceremonies. The patrician building of the 14th century, the best example

The facade of Palazzo Davanzati with its typical loggia.

of which is the **Palazzo Davanzati**, built by the Davizzi around 1330, has by now lost all pretense of being an offensive or defensive structure. The size kept increasing, where possible, and the ground plan of the palaces expanded to include courtyards and even small green areas inside. The revetment, of rusticated *pietra forte* for the lower floors, became smoother on the upper part where rhythmic rows of arched windows were inserted. The typical «Florentine» arch consisted of a round-headed or flat intrados and a slightly pointed extrados. See for example the **Palazzo Salviati-Quaratesi** in the Via Ghibellina, corner Via Matteo Palmieri; the **Palazzo Canigiani**, in the Via dei Bardi; **Palazzo Salviati**, in the Via della Vigna Vecchia.

At the end of the 14th century Florence as a city was divided into three fairly distinct areas. The building fabric of the oldest part of the city, whose layout was originally Roman but partly modified in the early Middle Ages, was extremely dense, characterized by the presence of numerous tower houses and the emergence of large construction yards involved in the building of the principal religious centers (Duomo and Baptistery), political centers (Palazzo della Signoria) and economic centers (headquarters for the Guilds, Orsanmichele). The area included between the «*cerchia antica*» and the 12th-century belt of city walls was also the seat of intensive building activity, but its town plan was less fragmented, the streets tended to follow the routes established by the old *borghi* and formed an irregular network with a logic all its own, which depended on its «organic» origin. The building fabric, at least some of which had been formed in the 13th and 14th centuries, is characterized by the existence of patrician structures and was polarized around the city's main churches (*San Pier Maggiore, San Lorenzo, Santa Trinita, Santa Felicita*) as well as the ensemble of *Badia-Palazzo del Podestà*. Lastly the more recent urban area, which stretched up to the new city walls, also seemed to have been laid down along the roads of the *borghi* which were once «*extra moenia*», and was organized into quarters centered around the churches of the principal convents of the mendicant orders (*Santa Croce, Santa Maria Novella, Santissima Annunziata-San Marco, Santo Spirito, Carmine, Ognissanti*). The most common types of buildings here were modest dwellings arranged in long rows on either side of the roads. These small houses were only four or five meters wide but were well developed in depth, and included small vegetable or flower gardens. Near the walls there were large holdings of ecclesiastic institutions or wealthy citizens which were used for vegetable farms or extensive gardens. Reminiscences of these green spaces, or what is left of them in the form of clusters of trees, can still be found in the toponymy of the city: Via dell'Ortone, Via dell'Orto, Via dell'Ulivo, Via della Pergola, Via della Rosa, Via del Fico, Canto agli Aranci, etc. Not to mention the streets that later changed their names such as Via Sant'Agostino (formerly Via degli Allori), Via degli Alfani (part of which was called Via del Ciliegio), Via dell'Orto dei Servi (now Via Gino Capponi), etc. The various parts of the city, despite their differences, comprised a fairly compact ensemble, where whatever the functional specialization of some of the zones may have been did not result in disintegration, for that «integration on a microurbanistic level (a coinciding of working and living quarters), which was gradually to diminish from the 15th century on» (G. Fanelli) prevailed.

Giovanni di Bicci dei Medici in an old portrait by Bronzino.

THE FIFTEENTH CENTURY

When power returned to the *popolo grasso* at the end of the 14th century, an oligarchic regime was established in Florence and a small restricted number of the merchant middle class governed the city for about 40 years and fostered an extremely active foreign policy, costly as far as the continuous wars were concerned, but nevertheless capable of halting the expansionism of the Visconti and of considerably enlarging the territory of the city-state by conquering Arezzo, Cortona, Prato, Pistoia and Pisa. The fact that Florence had Pisa and its ports (Porto Pisano and then Livorno) at its complete disposition made her a sea power and the uncontested «most complete and most perfect economic power of the West» (Y. Renouard). One of the consequences, internally, of the considerable costs of financing the wars was a reform of the tax system which led to the institution of the *Catasto* or Land Register (1427), a device by which it was theoretically possible to tax everyone according to their means, taking into account the conspicuous wealth in real estate which had previously been practically exempt. These same years witnessed a growing opposition to the oligarchy which was to ably exploit the malcontent of the populace. That part of the middle class which had been excluded from power joined arms with the people and found a leader in Giovanni de' Medici, head of the richest and most powerful company of Calimala. After the death of Giovanni (1429) the contrast was accentuated while the current of opinion favorable to the Medici continued to grow. The oligarchists headed by Rinaldo degli Albizi tried to eliminate Cosimo, Giovanni's firstborn, with defamatory accusations, but they only succeeded in sending him into exile (1433) from which he was recalled only a year later by a new Signoria that was favorable to him. From this moment on Cosimo was lord of the city, although he attempted to conceal the fact, leaving the old republican institutions intact, but emptied of any effective power. The last of the great city-states in central Italy, Florence, too, fell under the power of a single man, and it was the beginning of the principality which however did not formally take the place of the republic until about a hundred years later, in 1530. Cosimo, who died in 1464, was followed by the mediochre Piero the Gouty (1464-1469) whose son, Lorenzo the Magnificent, was to continue his ancestor's dissimulating policy up almost to the end of the century, maintaining the traditional offices, but with no doubts as to what he was to all effects: the true lord of Florence.

During the years in which the merchant oligarchy governed Florence and in the early period of Medici rule, the increasingly frequent contacts with examples of Greek and Roman antiquity gave rise to a new spirit and the city became the center in which Humanism was forged. Man considered himself the ultimate end, eager for rational knowledge and bent on affirming his dominion over the nature which surrounded him and the history which preceded him. Literary culture, the sciences, arts and human activities in their entirety attain a complete spiritual fusion, in a unique equilibrium which forgathers artists, craftsmen and scientists in a single platonic ideal of eternal truth and beauty. Filippo Brunelleschi's activity falls at the dawn of this golden period in European intellect and culture. Between 1420 and 1446 he created a group of works which were to represent one of the most important moments in the history of Florentine architecture and town-planning. Brunelleschi's works take their place in the urban framework which can be traced to Arnolfo di Cambio and which the city had inherited from the late Middle Ages. Synthetically they might be considered a «modernization» of medieval buildings. But the inventive power and newness of vision inherent in the work of the great Florentine architect were such as to lead to the affirmation in medieval Florence of a new rational order which transforms any pre-existing meaning. It is then thanks first of all to Brunelleschi and secondly to the other exponents of the architectural culture of the early 15th century that Florence, while maintaining its urban layout of the late Middle Ages practically intact, was to present itself from then on as the «Renaissance city» *par excellence*, idealized by the humanists.

In his *Panegirico della città di Firenze*, Leonardo Bruni exclaimed: «and what is there so splendid or magnificent in all the world that can compare with the buildings of this city? Truly, every time I think of this comparison, I am ashamed of the other cities; even though some are embellished with one or two streets, but the rest are empty and lacking in ornament». Benedetto Dei in his *Cronica fiorentina* was to echo him: «Lovely Florence has seven things and is endowed with each of them and no city can be called perfect unless it has all seven of them. First she has complete freedom, second she has a goodly number of wealthy and well dressed citizens, third she has a wide river of sweet water and mills within, fourth she is lord of the city and castles and lands and peoples and communes, fifth she has learning from Greek to the abacus and sixth every art in its entirety and perfection, seventh and last she has banks and firms throughout the world and neither Venetian nor Milanese nor Genovese nor Neapolitan nor Senese can compare».

The first example of Brunelleschi's exceptional architectural ability was to be the **dome of Santa Maria del**

Fiore which was begun in 1426 without the use of centering, adopting instead a system of masonry consisting of interlocking or herringbone courses of bricks which counteracted their own thrust so that the dome was able to hold itself up during the building. Work went on continuously, despite the difficulties and the polemics suscitated by the novelty of the building system Brunelleschi had invented, and came to an end in 1436 with the closing of the central oculus. In the same year the admirable lantern of the dome was begun, following a model which Brunelleschi had previously prepared in 1432 after winning a competition. The dome consisted of two concentric shells, whose slightly pointed form took into consideration the thrusts of the Gothic ribbing but within the framework of a new technical-formal vision, which led to the conclusion of a building dating to another period, transforming its meaning. Indeed, with his dome Brunelleschi redefined Arnolfo's cathedral which had been conceived of as a long body that «opens out» into a great articulated octagonal tribune, and transformed «into proportions the building conceived in a dimensional sense». «With the full body of the dome he coordinates and concludes the spaces which radiate out from the choir and with its silhouette it balances in height the longitudinal space of the three aisles, with the convergence of the ribs he perspectively defines the form of the dome; this no longer weighs down on the building, but floats filled with air, with the elastic tension of the sections of masonry stretched taut between the ribs» (G.C. Argan). Leon Battista Alberti, perfectly aware of the construction's ideological and urbanistic meaning, was to define the dome as «a structure so great, rising up above the skies, so vast that it can cover with its shadow all the peoples of Tuscany». The project for the **Loggia of the Ospedale degli Innocenti**, the construction of which Brunelleschi superintended between 1421 and 1424, went on almost contemporaneously with the beginning of the work on the dome. The Loggia was first of all conceived of as part of the city plan, as an inherent part of the overall scheme of the square in front of the church of the Servi di Maria, and not as an isolated structure. The original plans already called for an analogous portico on the other side of the square, with the facade of *Santissima Annunziata* in the background framed by the two loggias. The function of Brunelleschi's Loggia was therefore distinct from that of the porticoes of the other Florentine hospitals and the facade belonged as much to the piazza as to the building itself. Set on a base consisting of nine steps, the airy round-headed arches springing from slender Corinthian columns scan the facade. They define the front elevation with its series of windows with classical triangular pediments. The light entablature is terminated laterally by pilasters, while some years later (circa 1463), with a finishing touch of exquisite decorative grace, ten tondos in glazed terracotta by Andrea della Robbia were inserted in the spandrils. Particularly evident in the decorative elements of the loggia (capitals, pediments, molding) are the bonds with the classicism that was typical of the Florentine Romanesque and in which Brunelleschi spied «*qualche cosetta di rifresso dello splendore di quelli antichi edifici di Roma*» (a reflection of the splendor of those ancient buildings of Rome). Another superb creation by Brunelleschi is the basilica of **San Lorenzo**, the reconstruction of which, promoted by the Medicis, began in 1419, was later interrupted, and not undertaken anew until 1442. It

was finished after the death of the master by Antonio Manetti, who was also responsible for the spacious cloister with two orders. The plan of the church, with a nave and two aisles and a projecting transept, is not very different from the traditional schemes, but inside the building Brunelleschi's architectural reform, with its essential features of order, measure, geometric clarity, are overwhelmingly evident. The rhythm of the arcades, springing from monolithic columns with Corinthian capitals, lacks the dynamism of Gothic interiors since the entire building «has been conceived and organized in relationship to the various points of view in which the visitor is likely to find himself». This is what gives the building its «anthropocentric» and therefore typically humanistic character which was to be even more completely expressed in two small central-plan buildings: the **Old Sacristy of San Lorenzo** and the *Pazzi Chapel*. The interior of the former is comprised of an exact square covered with a melon dome with a lantern and furnished with a small apse. The walls are articulated by an entablature with supporting elements and trim in *pietra serena* and the lunettes in the upper part, like the four pendentives at the corners, are filled in with medallions in polychrome stucco by Donatello. This small room represents one of the most perfectly balanced creations of the Renaissance, in the perfect fusion of the structural and ornamental elements, as well as the rigorous interdependence of the arrangment of the several parts. The same motif is taken in hand and more thoroughly studied in the **Pazzi Chapel** in *Santa Croce*, begun two years after the *Old Sacristy of San Lorenzo* and continued after Brunelleschi's death. Preceded by a classicizing portico on six Corinthian columns in *pietra serena* which support an attic divided into panels, the Chapel also demonstrates how the Master prodigiously continued to renew his art. The central plan layout was also to return in another building which however remained incomplete: **Santa Maria degli Angioli**. Inspired by the classic «rotundas», the church was to have been an octagonal structure covered by a dome and surrounded by rectangular chapels with twin apses which would have given it a sixteen-sided exterior perimeter in which niches alternated with flat walls.
The most significant expression of Brunelleschi's mature style, in which his interest centers ever more on the plastic power of the architectural arrangement of the several parts, was to be **Santo Spirito**, designed in 1436 and, at least in part, unfaithfully executed after the artist's death. The church, in Latin cross plan, has a nave and two aisles separated by Corinthian columns which move around into the crossing and into the apse so as to create a continuos portico. The interior provides an effect of perfect harmony, with its play of arches and vaults, and with the flight of columns, twice as many as in *San Lorenzo*, for half columns also separate the apsidal chapels. These chapels, in the form of narrow high niches, were to have formed a series of apsidioles on the exterior, creating an unbroken succession of semi-cylindrical elements. They were however hidden by a flat wall by Antonio Manetti, Giovanni da Gaiole and Salvi d'Andrea who finished this last work of Brunelleschi's.
Brunelleschi's architectural message was carried on in the extremely personal style of Leon Battista Alberti who left some of his major works in Florence, examples of a completely unrhetorical re-evocation of the severity and grandiosity of the Romans, inserted into a

rigorous architectural context dominated by a deep-seated feeling for geometric eurythmy.

Between 1456 and 1470 Alberti realized the **facade of Santa Maria Novella**, completing the marble casing begun a century before. The artist brilliantly managed to reconcile the old and the new, grafting his work onto the two-color scheme typical of the Florentine Romanesque tradition, but reinterpreting it in the light of the new Renaissance taste. The Romanesque-Gothic decorations of the lower part were continued by a wide band scanned by marble intarsia squares and bordered by the heraldic sails of the Rucellai who had commissioned the work. Then, with two large sinuous volutes turned upside down he joined the masses at the sides to the center, which was divided by four pilasters and terminated by a triangular pediment, inside which was inserted the intarsia with the circular monogram of the name of Christ, echoing the oculus underneath. The broad main portal is also by Alberti. It is clearly classical in inspiration and of an extreme purity of form in its measured ornament.

Around 1467, at the behest of Giovanni Rucellai, Alberti designed the **Shrine of the Holy Sepulcher** for the Rucellai Chapel that was part of the church of **San Pancrazio**, (the classicizing facade is also his). The small rectangular temple is encased in two-color marble facing in geometric designs, separated by elegant Corinthian pilaster strips. The high trabeation of the shrine is crowned by an exotic crenellation of Florentine lilies which imitates orientalizing crenels while the whole structure is surmounted by a lantern in Arabian style. In the same year the artist designed the **tribune of Santissima Annunziata**, in an attempt to solve the problem of grafting a hemispherical dome onto a longitudinal structure. To terminate the building Alberti invented a sanctuary comprised of a large rotonda with faceted external walls with nine protruding chapels which dilate the large central area covered by a dome. Various other outstanding artistic personalities in 15th-century Florence departed from Bunelleschi's stylistic idiom and created an original architecture of their own. These include Il Cronaca who designed the church of **San Giuseppe** (done in collaboration with Baccio d'Agnolo) and who was also the architect for **San Salvatore al Monte**, called «*bella villanella*» by Michelangelo, where the «severity of the structure, typological innovations and premanneristic ferments»

are perfectly integrated; Bernardo Rossellino whose works include the termination of the **large cloister of Santa Croce**, the plan for which can be attributed to Brunelleschi, and the **Chiostro degli Aranci** in the **Badia Fiorentina**; Giuliano da San Gallo, author of the **Sacristy of Santo Spirito**, who created a prototype of a single nave church in **Santa Maria Maddalena de' Pazzi**, where square chapels covered with domical vaults lead off the nave; Antonio Manetti, who renewed the church of **San Felice** and built the **Chapel of the Cardinal of Portugal** in **San Miniato al Monte**. The most outstanding figure however is Michelozzo who took over the reconstruction of the **Convent of San Marco** when, with the suppression of the order of the Silvestrini, it passed to the Dominicans. Of particular note among the numerous rooms in the Convent, which follows the traditional plan of the monastic complex, are the so-called **Chiostro di Sant'Antonino**, on Ionic columns and with cross vaulting, and the elegant **library**, divided into three aisles by a succession of arches on slender columns which are also Ionic.

Michelozzo's activity brings us to the numerous interventions in civil architecture which in the course of the 15th century transformed the fabric of Florentine building, albeit not uniformly. Brunelleschi's influence was felt here too. His was the design on which, beginning in 1440, the construction of **Palazzo Pitti** was based. Originally the building consisted of just the central block, with two stories and arches on the ground floor. Although the rustication of the facing still echoed the medieval palace-fortress, the regularity of the relationship, calculated on the basis of the «golden section», and the calm rhythm of the openings «reveal a lucid ordered mentality». In precedence (1435) Brunelleschi had completed the **Palazzo di Parte Guelfa**, building a tall first floor with large round-arched windows resting on a molded entablature on the pre-existing bottom part. But it was above all Michelozzo who was to define, on the basis of Brunelleschi's experience, the 15th-century canons of the patrician dwelling, particularly in the **Medici Palace** built in the Via Larga (and later taken over by the Riccardi). From now on the palace was to spread out in a regular ground plan with the rooms arranged around an ample courtyard surrounded by loggias.

Michelozzo was the point of reference for Giuliano da Sangallo in the **Palazzo Gondi**, and for Giuliano da

S. Maria degli Angeli, or « La Rotonda », by Brunelleschi.

Palazzo Guadagni in Piazza S. Spirito.

Above, left: the Palazzo di Parte Guelfa; right: the Palazzo Antinori. Below: the facade of the Palazzo Rucellai.

Maiano, to whom the **Palazzo Antinori** is attributed. The most important Florentine palace of the Renaissance (the monumental **Palazzo Strozzi**), the work of Benedetto da Maiano, is also clearly derived from Brunelleschi and Michelozzo as was generally also the case for the numerous other patrician dwellings realized in the course of the 15th century: **Palazzo Corsi** (later Horne) in the Via dei Benci and **Palazzo Dei** (later Guadagni) in the Piazza Santo Spirito, both by Il Cronaca; **Palazzo Pazzi** (later Quaratesi) in the Via del Proconsolo, perhaps by Giuliano da Maiano, etc. Leon Battista Alberti, in turn, in realizing the **Palazzo Rucellai** for the Rucellai family, created a more refined type of patrician dwelling, with a revetment of ashlars in place of the rusticated masonry, and with a vertical division by pilaster strips which was added on to the horizontal subdivisions. Classic reminiscences abound: the fake *opus reticulatum* in the base, the doors with lintels, the superimposition of the orders (the pilaster strips on the ground floor have Doric capitals, those on the next story are Ionic and those on the top story are Corinthian).

Throughout the 15th century private building activity prevailed and numerous patrician structures, the expression of the growing power of the bourgeois merchant class, were scattered throughout the city. The principal families who initiated the building program with their palaces conceived of their presence in a given urban area as a symbol of their prestige and of the new political role they had acquired under the oligarchy. Thus the families of the Medici, the Pitti, the Rucellai, the Strozzi, the Gondi, the Guadagni intended their mansions to be a «monument which in its size and its qualification as a monument, in the quality of the design which also involved a revival of classic elements, was capable of affirming the role and power of the family to whom it belonged» (G. Fanelli).

THE SIXTEENTH CENTURY

Lorenzo the Magnificent knew how to impose his personal power without overthrowing the republican institutions. He likewise also managed to establish a certain equilibrium between the various Italian states, avoiding intervention by the great foreign powers. But upon his death (1492) it took only a few years for the son who succeeded him, Pietro the Unlucky, to demolish the wonderful structure of Medici power. The cowardly policy of Pietro regarding the invader Charles VIII constrained the city to eliminate him and reestablish in full the republican regime. But the people were divided between those who sided with the Medici, the great families who wanted to restore an oligarchic government, and the bulk of citizens, inflamed by the sermons of Girolamo Savonarola, a Dominican friar from San Marco, one of the highest expressions of the religious tradition in the city. Savonarola's followers reformed the government, imposing a new regime in which an important role was given to a «Gran Consiglio» which reunited the members of the principal families. But it was not long before the Medicis and their supporters made a comeback, thanks to the fact that Savonarola had been judged a heretic and burned at the stake in the Piazza della Signoria on May 23, 1498 on the order of Pope Alexander VI against whom the friar's violent

sermons were directed. After a brief period in which the patrician republic was strengthened with the election of Pier Soderini as gonfalonier for life, the city once more found itself under Medici rule, at the behest of the pope, allied with the king of Aragon whose word was law in Italy after the departure of the king of France. The elevation to the papal throne, first of Giovanni de' Medici (Leo X), and then of Giulio (Clement VII) seemed to reinforce the Medici signoria even more. But when news of the sack of Rome (1527) arrived, the people rebelled and once more ousted the Medici and proclaimed their freedom. This was the last desperate attempt to reinstate the republican government. On August 12, 1530, after an eleven-month siege, the armies of the emperor and the pope together entered Florence and the following year, with imperial concession, Alexander de' Medici was declared «head of the government and of the state». The new lord, whom a subsequent resolution was to call «Duke of the Florentine Republic», installed a tyranny, with new institutions all under his control, and began a foreign policy of alliances with the most important reigning families in Europe, marrying a natural daughter of Emperor Charles V and giving his stepsister Caterina as wife to the second son of Francis I.

The adversaries of the Medici, headed by Filippo Strozzi, who had been forced into exile, tried in vain to overturn Duke Alessandro's government. They were unsuccessful even when Lorenzino (or Lorenzaccio) de' Medici assassinated Alessandro in 1537. At that time the best they could do was call in as successor Cosimo il Giovane, son of Giovanni delle Bande Nere, a younger branch of the family, since the line of Cosimo the Elder had been extinguished. Barely seventeen, the new duke however managed to command respect and gradually installed an autocratic regime. He also succeeded in crushing the adverse factions and reinforcing the state, bringing Siena under Florentine rule (1555). The state Cosimo now ruled over was regional, something republican Florence had never managed to achieve. He obtained a sovereign title from the pope and on March 5, 1570 was crowned grand duke of Tuscany by Pius V.

In the early decades of the century as the Medici were consolidating their power, they promoted various interventions in the city which centered around the church of *San Lorenzo*, traditionally tied to the family. Cardinal Giulio de' Medici (future Clement VII) had Michelangelo built the **Laurentian Library** (1523-1529) and the *New Sacristy* (1520-1534) which was to become the family mausoleum. The former, created to house the rich library founded by Cosimo the Elder and enlarged by Lorenzo the Magnificent, consists of a hall and a vestibule or «*ricetto*». The walls of the latter, high and narrow, are decorated on two orders with a magnificent decoration which heralds the Baroque. Massive coupled columns imprisoned in the wall alternate with blind windows (the light comes from above). At the center is the monumental and original tripartite staircase which leads to the austere elongated rectangular hall, the walls of which are scanned by a succession of windows and dark pilaster strips in sandstone which stand out against the white background.

The **New Sacristy** is to all effects a Medici funerary chapel. Square in plan and covered by a dome, the construction of the supports and trim in *pietra serena* against the light-colored walls seems to echo Brunelleschi's sacristy next door, but Michelangelo's concept is quite different. The members of the upper story are much lighter and slenderer so as to put the stress on the sepulchers below, which contain the mortal remains of Giuliano, third son of Lorenzo the Magnificent, and of Lorenzo II, son of Pietro the Unlucky. In the same way the architectural decorative elements of the ground floor gravitate towards the center of the walls where the funerary complexes are located, also by the hand of Michelangelo. The wonderful figures carved on the sarcophagi are elements in a symbolic language that centers on the statues of the two figures placed in niches above the urns.

Unlike Cosimo the Elder, who had governed the city in terms of advice and counsel (even though effectively his word was law), Cosimo I, from the beginning of his long government (1537-1574), attempted to render his absolute rule official with the aid of architecture and town planning. His purpose was to augment the prestige of the state, which was identified with the ruler. The characteristics of the patron-artist relationship therefore changed and artists were no longer commissioned by the community but acted on the precise behest of the absolute prince whose wishes they had to interpret. Consequently the new and important architectural realizations such as the modifications of the town plan, were an inherent part of the grand duke's cultural policy, aimed at affirming the greatness of the state. In 1540, significantly, the Medici residence was transferred from the palace in the Via Larga to the *Palazzo della Signoria*, which was enlarged and internally modified. A few years later (1550) the court moved to the *Palazzo Pitti*, which in turn was enlarged and transformed. Then in 1560 work was begun on the seat of the Medici magistrature, the **Uffizi**, a manifest architectural symbol of the new organization of an absolutist state. The subsequent construction of what is known as «**Vasari's Corridor**» to connect the *Palazzo della Signoria* with the *Palazzo Pitti* was the last step in the establishment of a real governative area in the heart of the city, within the framework of an incipient zoning of the urban fabric.

Vasari was the artist who best corresponded to Cosimo I's intentions. At his behest, besides the new buildings (*Uffizi*, «*Corridor*», *Logge del Pesce in Mercato Vecchio*), he was involved in the remodernization of a whole series of buildings (interior of the *Palazzo Vecchio* and the churches of *Santa Croce* and *Santa Maria Novella*), a result of the grand duke's aspirations to transform and embellish the city so it could rise to «expressions of the regal power and the greatness of the state». His architectural designs were obviously inspired by Michelangelo even when, with a genial town planning solution, he designed the grand complex of the **Uffizi**, with a long narrow piazza flanked by the facades of two severe building blocks which are joined together at the back so as to form a triumphal arch which leads directly to the right bank of the Arno. Another architect of the grand ducal workshops was Bartolomeo Ammannati who in 1560 was commissioned to enlarge and finish the **Palazzo Pitti**. Brunelleschi's original building was to all intents and purposes destroyed, with the proportions completely falsified, but in the courtyard Ammannati created what may well be his most significant work. Closed on three sides by the palace and on the fourth by a terraced ground floor which communicates with the **Boboli garden**, the courtyard is an original interpretation, already mannerist in style, of the rustication on the facade. In the

background, almost like a stage prop, is the vision of the garden above, begun in 1550 by Tribolo, continued by Ammannati and then by Buontalenti, Parigi and others. In those same years the artist contributed to the installation of the Piazza della Signoria, with his monumental *Fountain of Neptune*, together with Giambologna. Then, between 1567 and 1570, he created his other main work, the **Santa Trinita bridge**, which replaced the medieval structure that had been destroyed in the disastrous flood of 1557. «Masterpiece of both technique and style» the new bridge is characterized by its three elegant flattened arches, and the tautness of the special «catenary» line which reduced to a minimum the thickness of the thoroughfare.

Among other works promoted by Cosimo I mention at least should be made of the construction of the **Logge del Mercato Nuovo** (1547-1551), a broad elegant structure by Giovan Battista Del Tasso, as well as the reinforcement of the city's defenses which, among other things, led to the lowering of most of the towers on the city gates and to the construction of bastions and the amplification of the fortifications with which Michelangelo had surrounded the hill of San Miniato during the siege of 1529. Many examples of «urban furnishing», aimed at qualifying determined sites, were also realized. See for example the columns erected in the piazzas of San Marco, Santa Trinita and San Felice (at present only the one in the Piazza Santa Trinita is still standing), or the monuments, the tabernacles, the fountains, or even simply the coats of arms or the busts set on the buildings in homage to the grand duke. The presence of all these elements is significant and it reveals the affirmation of a hierarchy of the city streets and a renovation of the buildings along some of them (Via Maggio, Via dei Servi, Via Tornabuoni, Borgo degli Albizi, Via Santo Spirito, Via dei Ginori) which had become the principal routes in the 16th-century town plan.

Religious architecture was much less vital in the 16th century which was marked throughout by the completion of extant buildings (as was the case with the church of *Santo Spirito* which was enriched with two cloisters, respectively by Ammannati and by Parigi), or by their renovation (besides *Santa Croce* and *Santa Maria Novella*, the churches of *Santa Maria Maggiore*, *Santa Trinita*, *San Marco*, the *Carmine, Ognissanti, San Michele in Visdomini*, etc. were transformed). There were few new constructions and those that did go up were of modest dimensions: see **San Giovannino dei Cavalieri**, begun by Ammannati in 1579 and then completed by Parigi, the church of **Sant'Agata**, by Alessandro Allori (1592-1593), the so-called church of the **Pretoni** by Balducci, as well as the small churches of **San Niccolò del Ceppo**, by Giambologna (1561-1563) and **San Tommaso d'Aquino**, by Santi di Tito (1568). On the other hand activity in the field of private architecture with the construction of patrician dwellings was intense. In addition to the so-called «town villas» (*Pitti, Casino Mediceo*), new palaces were built by the new category of government officials and bureaucrats. On the whole this was a traditional architecture and resulted in severe and rigorously elegant palaces, works by Ammannati (**Palazzo Giugni** in the Via degli Alfani; **Palazzo Ramirez de Montalvo**, in the Borgo degli Albizi, with sgraffiti by Poccetti on the facade; **Palazzo Grifoni**, in the Piazza Santissima Annunziata), by Giovanni Dosio (**Palazzina Giacomini-Larderel**, in the Via Tornabuoni and **Palazzo dell'Arcivescovado**),

Left: the Palazzo Cocchi in Piazza S. Croce. Below: the Casino Mediceo in Via Cavour. At the foot of the page: the Loggia del Mercato Nuovo. Following page: the Palazzetto del Forte di Belvedere.

by Santi di Tito (**Palazzo Dardinelli**, in the Via Cavour), by Baccio d'Agnolo (**Palazzo Taddei**, in the Via Ginori; **Palazzo Cocchi**, in the Piazza Santa Croce; **Palazzo Ciaini**, in the Via dei Servi). Baccio d'Agnolo in particular developed a simplified type of patrician mansion with a loggia over the roof and with much of the rustication replaced by plastering. This type was to become very popular as can be seen in numerous other 16th-century palaces: see the **Palazzo Gerini**, in the Via Ginori; the **Palazzo Ginori**, in the street of the same name; the **Palazzo Capponi**, in the Via Santo Spirito; the **Palazzo Altoviti**, in the Borgo degli Albizi, called «*dei Visacci*» (of those awful faces) because the facade was ornamented with fifteen herms of illustrious Florentines.

An exceptional example of Roman taste and monumentality appears in the **Palazzo Pandolfini**, in the Via Sangallo, designed by Raphael in 1520 and carried out by Aristotile da Sangallo. Raphaelesque reminiscences also come to the fore in the facade of the **Palazzo Uguccioni**, in the Piazza della Signoria, by Matteo Folfi, and in the **Palazzo Batolini-Salimbeni**, in the Piazza Santa Trinita, by Baccio d'Agnolo, in the facade of which niches and cross mullioned windows flanked by columns alternate in projecting molding. The theme of the «town villa» begun with the *Pitti Palace* and the adjacent *Boboli gardens*, was continued with the realization of the so-called **Casino Mediceo**, built in 1574 for Don Antonio de' Medici. The building introduces us to the work of Bernardo Buontalenti, successor to Vasari and Ammannati in the grand ducal workyards. The multifaceted activity of this artist resulted in the creation of a whole series of architectural structures where a great simplicity and purity of form are not infrequently joined by curious decorative details which border on the grotesque. In the *Casino Mediceo* he created an enormous building which spread out horizontally. The smooth plastered walls are scanned by the ordered arrangement of the sparse

windows which are decorated on the ground floor by capricious brackets and shells. Outstanding among Buontalenti's other examples of civic architecture, including various palaces in the city (as well as the famous villas built in the country for the Medici: Artimino, Ambrogiana, etc.), is the **Palazzo Nonfinito**, which he began in 1592 for Alberto Strozzi and which was then continued by Caccini and Cigoli. An unusually monumental example of Renaissance civic architecture in Florence, the building is an exemplary expression of late 16th-century Florentine architectural culture, still bound to the canons of the best Renaissance tradition and loath to accept new experiments under way in Rome which had by then become the principal Italian center of intellectual and artistic life. Buontalenti's enormous production also includes the **Fortezza di Santa Maria del Belvedere**, built at the behest of Grand Duke Ferdinando I between 1590 and 1595. The scope of the structure was more that of dominating than defending the city as the position of the fort, with its star-shaped ground plan and skillfully articulated high bastions tell us. But the most unique aspect of the Fort, important from an artistic point of view, is the **Palazzina** at the top, with its irregular yet harmonious arrangement of the sober openings and with the invention of the double trabeated loggia which faces in two directions. The *Forte del Belvedere* is also the complement to another fortress, built in 1534-1535 in correspondence to the northwest stretch of walls. It was called **Fortezza di San Giovanni Battista**, later known as «**da Basso**» or «lower» to distinguish it from the Belvedere which was «higher» over the city. It was designed by Antonio da Sangallo and carried out by Alessandro Vitelli and Pier Francesco da Viterbo. The enormous imposing structure is pentagonal in plan with bastions reinforcing the corners. At the beginning of the Medici rule it was a real stronghold which the first dynasts had built so they would have a safe refuge in the case of uprisings.

THE RELIGIOUS CENTERS

CHURCH OF S. CROCE

Inside it contains the *funeral monuments* of famous people in the world of art and culture and numerous chapels, including the **Bardi Chapel** with frescoes by Giotto. The **Pazzi Chapel** overlooks the **Cloister**.

MUSEO DELL'OPERA DI S. CROCE

Inside the Cloister of the Basilica, it houses Gaddi's fresco with the *Tree of the Cross* and Cimabue's famous *Crucifix*.

CHURCH OF S. MARIA NOVELLA

Facade of the Church by Alberti. Inside: frescoes by Ghirlandaio — in the **Cappella Maggiore** — and the large *Last Judgement* — in the **Cappella degli Strozzi di Mantova**.

SPANISH CHAPEL

In the convent of S. Maria Novella, decorated inside with *frescoes* by Andrea di Bonaiuto.

CHURCH OF S. LORENZO

Basilica on the site of the oldest city church. Inside: the splendid *bronze pulpits* by Donatello and Brunelleschi's **Old Sacristy**.

MEDICI CHAPELS (Piazza Madonna degli Adobrandini)

Inside: the vast subterranean chamber, the sumptuous **Chapel of the Princes** with the Medici sepulchers and the **New Sacristy** by Michelangelo.

CHURCH OF SS. ANNUNZIATA

Church of the Servites. Inside: the **Chiostrino dei Voti**, the **Tabernacle of the Annunziata** and the **Chiostro dei Morti**.

PIAZZA SS. ANNUNZIATA

Symmetrically laid out picturesque piazza. On either side, the **porticoes** of the **Confraternita dei Servi di Maria** and of the **Ospedale degli Innocenti**. At the center Tacca's **Fountains** and the **Equestrian statue of Ferdinando I de' Medici**.

CHURCH OF S. MINIATO AL MONTE (Viale Galileo Galilei)

Situated near Piazzale Michelangelo. Inside: fascinating **Crypt**, the **presbytery** with its marvelous *mosaics* and the **Sacristy**. Outside: the **Monumental Cemetery** and the **Bishops' Palace**.

LESSER CHURCHES

Ognissanti Church: in the Refectory, Ghirlandaio's *Last Supper*.
In the Oltrarno: the **Church of S. Frediano in Cestello**, the **Church of S. Spirito** by Brunelleschi and the **Church of the Carmine**, with the fresco cycle by Masaccio in the **Brancacci Chapel**.
Also worthy of note: **S. Salvatore al Vescovo**, in the Piazza dell'Olio; the **Badia Fiorentina**, in the Via del Proconsolo; **S. Carlo dei Lombardi**, in the Via Calzaioli; **S. Salvi**, with the *Last Supper* by Andrea del Sarto; **SS. Apostoli** and **S. Gaetano** in the Piazza Antinori.
Inside the **Church of S. Trinita**, Ghirlandaio's important frescoes in the **Sassetti Chapel**.

Facing page: two views of S. Croce. Above: the interior of the basilica; right: the marble pulpit by Benedetto da Maiano.

CHURCH OF S. CROCE

This monument is truly unique, not only for the purity of the Gothic style, but also for the famous works of art it contains and its historical importance. The Basilica of Santa Croce, one of the largest churches in the city, is attributed to the genius of Arnolfo di Cambio who seems to have begun work in 1294. Work continued into the second half of the 14th century but the church was not consecrated until 1443. The facade with its three gables dates to the 19th century (project by N. Matas) and the **campanile** *in Gothic style also dates to this period (1847, project by G. Baccani). A portico of airy arches runs along the left flank and shelters the 14th-century tomb of Francesco Pazzi. On the right side of the church are the* **Cloisters**, *with the* **Pazzi Chapel** *in the background, and the* **Museo dell'Opera di S. Croce**. *The imposing interior has a nave and two side aisles separated by slender octagonal piers from which spring spacious pointed arches with a double molding. The beauty of the Church has been partially obfuscated by 16th-century remodelling. The floor is covered with old tombstones for the entire length of the nave which has a trussed timber ceiling. The transept has a number of chapels, including the* **Cappella Maggiore** *with the Legend of the Holy Cross (1380) by Agnolo Gaddi. On the altar is Gerini's polyptych with the Madonna and Saints and, above, the Crucifix of the school*

Facing page, above, left: funeral monument to Michelangelo; right: funeral monument to Galileo Galilei. Below: the Tabernacle of the Annunciation with a detail of the Angel, by Donatello. This page, above, left: funeral monument to Alfieri, the Italian poet, and, on the right, to Machiavelli. Below: the funeral monument to Dante Alighieri.

of Giotto. A Deposition from the Cross *(cartoon by Lorenzo Ghiberti)* in stained glass can be admired on the interior facade. *Below to the right is the* Monument to Gino Capponi *(1876), and to the left that to* G. B. Niccolini *(1883). A splendid marble* pulpit *by Benedetto da Maiano (1472-76) stands in the nave. To be noted in the right aisle, at the first altar, is a Crucifixion by Santi di Tito (1579); on the first pier is the famous bas-relief by Antonio Rossellino (1478) of the Madonna del Latte. The stained-glass windows date to the 14th century. The most famous funeral monuments are along the walls of the right aisle. These include the monument to Dante Alighieri by Ricci (1829); to Michelangelo, by Vasari (1579); to Alfieri, by Canova (1803); to Machiavelli, by I. Spinazzi (1787). Fragments of frescoes by Orcagna are to be seen behind the fourth altar and further on is Domenico Veneziano's fine fresco (1450) of St. John the Baptist and St. Francis. Next comes the tabernacle in pietra serena by Donatello and Michelozzo with the Annunciation (1435 c.) by Donatello. and then the Tomb of Leonardo Bruni by Bernardo Rossellino, the funeral monument to Rossini and the one to Foscolo. The right arm of the transept contains the* **Castellani Chapel** *superbly frescoed by Agnolo Gaddi (1385) with Stories of the Saints. On the altar a Crucifix by Gerini.*

In the facing page: the Cappella Maggiore of S. Croce. Right: the Bardi Chapel with the panel of S. Francis by an unknown 13th-century painter. Below: Giotto's fresco with the funeral of S. Francis.

At the end of the transept is the **Baroncelli Chapel**, with the splendid Gothic tomb of the Baroncelli family and a lunette with a Madonna by Taddeo Gaddi. The frescoes on the walls with Stories of Mary are also by Gaddi and the Madonna of the Girdle is by Bastiano Mainardi (1490). The Coronation of the Virgin on the altar is by Giotto. Michelozzo's portal leads to the **Sacristy**, with the **Rinuccini Chapel**, frescoed with Stories of the Magdalen and the Virgin by Giovanni da Milano. The fine altarpiece is by Giovanni del Biondo (1379). Michelozzo's **Medici Chapel**, built for Cosimo the Elder, is at the back. It contains a magnificent bas-relief by Donatello and various works by the Della Robbias. Various chapels (14th-cent.) with important works open off the central zone of the transept. These include the **Velluti Chapel** with Stories of St. Michael Archangel, perhaps by Cimabue; the **Chapels of the Peruzzi and the Bardi** families frescoed by Giotto with Stories of St. John the Evangelist (1320) and Stories of St. Francis (1318); the **Tosinghi Chapel** with the Assumption in Heaven, also by Giotto; the **Pulci Chapel** with frescoes by Bernardo Daddi. Of particular note in the left aisle is the Marsuppini Sepulcher by Desiderio da Settignano.

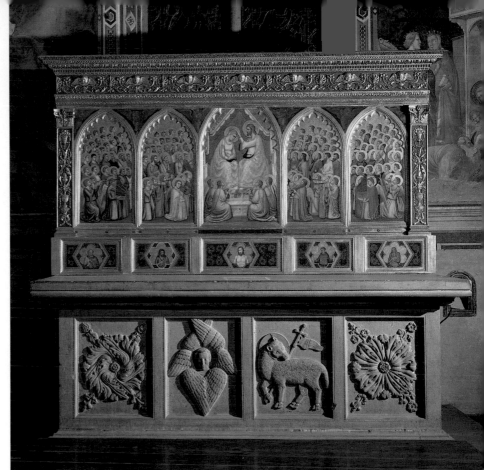

Facing page: the Baroncelli Chapel. This page, above, right: Giotto's panel of the Coronation of the Virgin, in the same chapel; below: the Castellani Chapel with the Crucifix by Niccolo di Pietro Gerini.

Above: the Sacristy with the Rinuccini Chapel. Facing page, above: Brunelleschi's dome on the Pazzi Chapel, and, below, the altar.

PAZZI CHAPEL AND MUSEO DI S. CROCE

At the back of the Basilica's **First Cloister** is the **Pazzi Chapel**, a daring example of Brunelleschi's genius, begun in 1443. The decorations are by Desiderio da Settignano, Luca della Robbia, Giuliano da Maiano. A pronaos or porch on Corinthian columns precedes the chapel. The cylindrical dome, with a conical roof and a round lantern, was finished in 1461. The interior is a jewel of Renaissance harmony with its white walls articulated by the grey stone pilaster strips. The **Museo dell'Opera di S. Croce** has been installed in the **Refectory**, to the right of the **Cloister**.

Above: the Refectory of S. Croce. Below, left: Cimabue's Crucifix and, on the right, a Della Robbia tabernacle in the Museum of S. Croce.

SANT E PATER BARTOLOMEE · ORA · PRO NOBIS

Above: the courtyard of the Cloister of S. Croce. Right: the statue of Dante on the steps of the Basilica of S. Croce.

MUSEO DI S. CROCE
The museum houses outstanding works of Florentine art from the 14th to the 16th centuries. Unfortunately the flood of 1966 seriously damaged some of them. The most famous, and the saddest, is Cimabue's great Crucifix hung on the right wall of the **Refectory** *(the enormous fresco with the Tree of the Cross and Scenes from the Lives of the Saints on the back wall is by Taddeo Gaddi). Even so the museum contains other masterpieces by Maso di Banco, Orcagna, Donatello, della Robbia, Veneziano, Bronzino.*

Above: the facade of S. Maria Novella. Left: one of the obelisks in the piazza. Facing page: two views of the Spanish Chapel.

CHURCH OF. S. MARIA NOVELLA
The Dominican friars, Sisto da Firenze and Ristoro da Campi, began to build the church in 1246 on the site of the 10th-century Dominican oratory of S. Maria delle Vigne. The nave and aisles went up in 1279 and the building was finished in the middle of the 14th century with the **campanile** and the **Sacristy** by Jacopo Talenti. The marvelous facade was remodelled between 1456 and 1470 by Leon Battista Alberti (the original facade was early 14th century) who created the splendid portal and everything above it, articulated in inlaid squares and bordered by the heraldic sails of the Rucellai family who commissioned the work. Two large reversed volutes tie the lateral masses together with those in the center, articulated by four engaged pilasters and terminating in a triangular pediment. The interior is divided into a nave and two aisles by compound piers with pointed arches, and 16th-century renovation.

CHURCH OF S. MARIA NOVELLA
INTERIOR
The church houses numerous works from the 14th to the 16th centuries. Of particular note are the Monument to the Beata Villana by Rossellino (1451); the Bust of St. Antoninus (in terra cotta) and the Tomb of the Bishop of Fiesole by Tino da Camaino; Ghiberti's lovely tombstone for Leonardo Dati (1423); the Tomb of Filippo Strozzi by Benedetto da Maiano 1491); Vasari's Madonna of the Rosary (1568); the Miracle of Jesus by Bronzino. Be sure

to stop for a while in the **Cappella Maggiore** *(or Tornabuoni Chapel)*, with a fine bronze Crucifix by Giambologna on the altar and frescoes with the Stories of St. John the Baptist *and* Stories of the Madonna *by Domenico Ghirlandaio, late 15th cent.); the* **Gondi Chapel**, *by Giuliano da Sangallo, with fragments of frescoes by 13th-century Greek painters on the vault and Brunelleschi's famous Crucifix on the back wall; the* **Cappella Strozzi di Mantova**, *with frescoes of the* Last Judgement *on the back wall,* Hell *on the right wall and* Paradise *on the left, by Nardo di Cione or Orcagna. The gate to the left of the facade leads to the* **First Cloister**, *in Romanesque style (1350) frescoed with* Scenes from the Old Testament *by Paolo Uccello (now in the* **Refectory***). From here, through the* **Chiostrino dei Morti**, *one arrives at the* **Chiostro Grande**, *with more than fifty arches and completely lined with frescoes by Florentine masters of the 15th and 16th centuries (generally not open to the public since it is now used by the armed forces).*

SPANISH CHAPEL

The old Chapter Hall *of the convent can be reached through the portal on the north side of the* **First Cloister** *(Chiostro Verde). Built by Jacopo Talenti (1359), in 1540 Eleonora of Toledo, Cosimo I's wife, took it over as her private chapel for the religious services of her court. It is completely lined with frescoes by Andrea di Bonaiuto (mid-14th cent.) which depict scenes inspired by the* Mirror of True Penitance *by the prior Jacopo Passavanti, exemplary apologia of the Dominican rule of St. Dominic and St. Thomas of Aquinas.*

Facing page, above: the two-color arcading enclosing the left side of S. Maria Novella; below: the Chiostro Grande. This page: two details of the Spanish Chapel.

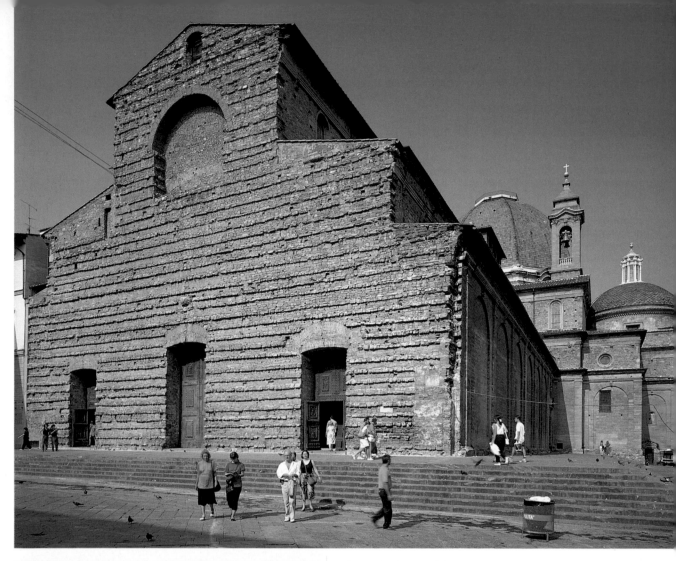

Above: the facade of the Church of S. Lorenzo. Left: the Cloister. Facing page, above: the interior of the church, and, below, one of the two bronze pulpits by Donatello.

CHURCH OF S. LORENZO
*This is the oldest church in the city (consecrated by St. Ambrose in 393) and it was rebuilt along Romanesque lines in 1060. What we see now is Brunelleschi's adaptation of 1423. The facade, magnificent and moving in its bareness, was supposed to be faced with marble (Michelangelo's project was never carried out). Of particular note inside, among others, are Donatello's two bronze pulpits and his choir-loft, as well as the **Old Sacristy**, Brunelleschi's first work (1419-28).*

MEDICI CHAPELS

The large complex, containing the tombs of the Medici, is just behind the Church of San Lorenzo. Various rooms and the vault are in common. From the entrance vestibule we enter a vast, low room, created by Buontalenti, where we can find the tombs of Donatello, Cosimo the Elder, members of the Lorraine dynasty *as well as other grand-ducal tombs. The staircase leads to the large **Chapel of the Princes**, created and begun by Nigetti (with additional touches by Buontalenti) in 1602; it was finished in the eighteenth century. The interior is octagonal in shape, completely clad in pietradura and marble in line with the Baroque taste; above the base with 16 coats-of-arms of the grand-ducal cities, there are six sarcophagi of the grand dukes* Cosimo III, Francesco I, Cosimo I, Ferdinando I, Cosimo II, Ferdinando II, *two of which have statues of the Grand Dukes by Tacca. A corridor leads from the Chapel of the Princes to the* **New Sacristy**.

Left: the cupola of the Chapel of the Princes. Below: a view of the animated Borgo S. Lorenzo. Facing page, above: the interior of the cupola of the Chapel of the Princes, and, below, the altar.

This page: the coats of arms of Florence, Pisa, and Siena inlaid in stone on the walls of the Chapel of the Princes. Facing page: details of Michelangelo's figures in the New Sacristy. Above, left: the tomb of Giuliano, duke of Nemours; right: the tomb of Lorenzo, duke of Urbino; below: the Madonna and Child between Saints Cosmas and Damian.

Facing each other on the following pages are, above, Night and Day, and below, Dusk and Dawn, works by Michelangelo set on the tombs of the two Medici dukes.

SACRESTIA NUOVA

The **New Sacristy***, entered from the* **Medici Chapels***, stands near the right transept of the* **Basilica of S. Lorenzo***. Created by Michelangelo (1520), it overturns Brunelleschi's concept of restrained balance with the dynamic rhythms of its decoration. The Sacristy contains Michelangelo's* Medici Tombs, *that of Giuliano, duke of Nemours, and of Lorenzo, duke of Urbino. The figures of* Day *and* Night *watch over the tomb of Giuliano and* Dusk *and* Dawn *over that of Lorenzo.*

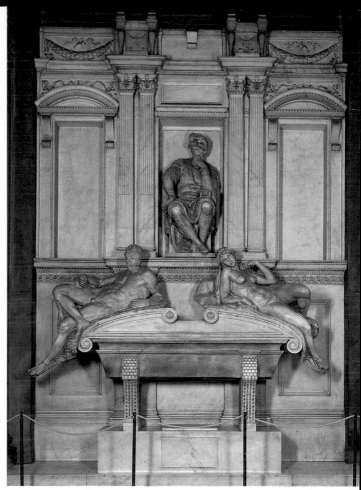

Above: the equestrian statue of Ferdinando I dei Medici in front of the Ospedale degli Innocenti. Below, left: one of the Fountains by Tacca and, on the right, one of the roundels Andrea della Robbia made for the Ospedale.

PIAZZA SS. ANNUNZIATA

After leaving the **Church of the SS. Annunziata**, *to the left is the complex of the* **Ospedale degli Innocenti** *(designed by Brunelleschi and finished by F. Luna in 1445). The facade presents a lovely portico of nine arches decorated with polychrome terra-cotta roundels of babes in swaddling clothes (it was a foundling home) by Andrea della Robbia (1463). Inside is a magnificent* **Courtyard** *and the first floor houses the* **Collection of detached frescoes** *and the* **Gallery of the Hospital**. *Across the square, opposite the Ospedale is the* **Portico of the Confraternità dei Servi di Maria**, *built by Sangallo the Elder and Baccio*

Above: the facade of the Church of SS. Annunziata. Right: the Chiostro dei Voti within the complex

d'Agnolo (1516-25) in imitation of Brunelleschi's portico. The equestrian statue of Ferdinando de' Medici stands at the center of the square. It is practically a twin to the one of Cosimo I in the Piazza della Signoria and was also by Giambologna although Tacca finished it (1608). The two Fountains symmetrically placed at the sides of the square are also by Tacca. They date to 1629 and were made for the port of Livorno.

CHURCH OF THE SS. ANNUNZIATA
Originally an oratory (1250) of the Order of the Servi di Maria, the building stood outside the second circle of city walls. Between 1444 and 1481 Michelozzo, Pagno Portinari and Antonio Manetti (with suggestions from L. B. Alberti) remodelled it into its present form. The facade has a portico on

Left, above: the interior of the Church of SS. Annunziata; below: a detail of the ceiling. Facing page: the Tabernacle of the Annunziata inside the church.

Corinthian columns. The central portal leads to the **Chiostrino dei Voti** (1447), a particularly scenographic space with lunettes frescoed by Rosso Fiorentino, Pontormo, Andrea del Sarto (1511-13). The interior, remodelled in the middle of the 17th century, has a single large nave with the arched openings of the chapels set on either side. To be noted is Volterrano's magnificent coffered ceiling (1664). Entrance to the **Chiostro dei Morti** (1453) with frescoes by Poccetti is to the left of the transept.

THE BAROQUE IN FLORENCE
In the field of architecture, the Baroque style did not produce that abundance of examples we can find in Rome. The best example of Baroque style is, without doubt, the **Chapel of the Princes** in San Lorenzo, built on designs by Don Giovanni de' Medici, Buontalenti and Nigetti who also worked on the **Church of San Gaetano** and on the facade of the **Church of Ognissanti**. In the interior of the **Church of SS. Annunziata** we can find a remarkable example of the Late Baroque of Roman extraction. As regards private buildings, the palaces of the noble Florentine families in the seventeenth century reveal little Baroque influence and continued to follow the dictates of the fifteenth and sixteenth centuries, as shown by the enlargements of the **Pitti**, **Medici-Riccardi** and **Capponi** Palaces.

Above: the facade of the Church of S. Miniato al Monte. Left: Michelozzo's Chapel of the Crucifix. Facing page: the interior of the church.

CHURCH OF S. MINIATO AL MONTE

*Bishop Hildebrand had the present structure built in 1018 on the site of a 4th-century chapel. The lower part of the facade is decorated by fine arcading; the upper part is simpler and has a fine 12th-century mosaic of Christ between the Madonna and St. Miniato. The church, with its unfinished **15th-century campanile** that was damaged during the siege of Florence in 1530, the **Bishop's Palace**, the **fortifications**, the **monumental cemetery** all stand at the top of a hill called Monte alle Croci, which rises up over the Piazzale Michelangelo below and over the entire city.*

CHURCH OF S. MINIATO
INTERIOR

*The interior of this magnificent example of Florentine Romanesque architecture (it originally belonged to the Benedictine monks and then passed to the Olivetan friars in 1373) is tripartite with a trussed timber roof. Outstanding is the pavement in the center with marble intarsias of signs of the zodiac and symbolic animals. The walls retain fragments of 13th- and 14th-century frescoes. Of note is the **crypt**, a vast space closed off by an elaborate wrought-iron gate (1338). The altar (11th-cent.) preserves the bones of St. Miniato. Fragments of frescoes by Taddeo Gaddi (1341) can be seen in the vaults of the crypt. The raised **presbytery** is of great beauty with its pulpit (1207) and an intimate choir with fine inlaid wooden choir stalls. The large mosaic of the Blessing*

Above: the mosaic with Christ Enthroned in the conch of the apse of S. Miniato. Below: the Crypt. Facing page: two views of the frescoes by Spinello Aretino in the Sacristy.

Christ flanked by the Madonna and Saints *(1297)* is in the conch of the apse. Entrance to the **Sacristy**, *completely frescoed by Spinello Aretino (1387) with the sixteen* Stories of the legend of St. Benedict, *is to the right of the presbytery. On the left, stairs lead to the* **Chapel of St. James**, *or « of the Cardinal of Portugal », designed by Antonio Manetti and decorated with five splendid roundels representing the* Holy Spirit *and the* Cardinal Virtues, *by Luca della Robbia (1461-66). To the right is the funeral monument of the Cardinal, a particularly lovely work by Antonio Rossellino (1461). The* **Chapel of the Crucifix**, *designed by Michelozzo, and with delicate glazed vaulting by Luca della Robbia, stands at the center of the church. To the right of the church is the* **Bishop's Palace** *(1295-1320), ancient summer residence of the bishops of Florence which then became a convent, a hospital and a Jesuit house.*

CENACOLO OF GHIRLANDAIO

One of Ghirlandaio's masterpieces is to be seen in the **Refectory** of the **Church of Ognissanti** (built in 1256 but thoroughly remodelled in the 17th cent.), after passing through Michelozzo's **Cloister**. This painting of the Last Supper (1480) is characterized by the new approach in describing the poses of the Apostles and the use of a landscape (delicate and serene) behind them. These elements may have influenced Leonardo da Vinci who saw the painting two years before leaving Florence.

CHURCH OF CESTELLO

The Church of S. Frediano in Cestello, even though the facade was never finished, is a rare example of the Baroque in Florence. It was built by Antonio Maria Ferri (on a design by the Roman Cerutti), 1680-89. The cupola on a drum (1698) is also his. Inside, the fine fresco in the cupola is by Gabbiani (1701-1718). The church is probably called Cestello because of the vicinity of Cosimo III's Granary, which stands on the eastern side of the square.

CHURCH OF S. SPIRITO

S. Spirito was meant by Brunelleschi to be a twin to S. Lorenzo, but the facade was never finished. The **dome** too is by Brunelleschi while the **campanile** is by Baccio d'Agnolo (1503). The interior is one of the finest examples of Renaissance architecture.

Left: the Church of Ognissanti. Below: Ghirlandaio's Last Supper in the Refectory adjacent to the church. Facing page, above: the Church of S. Frediano in Cestello, and, below, the Church of S. Spirito.

CHURCH OF THE CARMINE

The 14th-century church of S. Maria del Carmine was almost completely destroyed in a fire in 1771. The **Brancacci Chapel** in the right transept contains a fresco cycle painted between 1425 and 1428 by Masolino and, above all, by Masaccio (the Temptation is by the former; the famous Expulsion from Paradise and a series of scenes from the Life of St. Peter, including the well-known Tribute Money, are by the latter). The frescoes were finished by Filippino Lippi.

BRANCACCI CHAPEL: THE RESTORATION

The chapel preserves the most exalting cycle of frescoes known to western art, thanks to the presence of as extraordinary a painter as Masaccio who worked there from 1425 to 1427, in collaboration with Masolino, and the fact that it was finished more than 50 years later by Filippino Lippi. Recent restorations has eliminated retouching and over-painting of the past which had turned the colors into a heavy monochrome, and has restored the frescoes to what they originally were, where form, color and brilliance are marvellously balanced, as is evident in these two details taken from Masaccio's Tribute Money and Masolino's Resurrection of Tabitha.

Left: the facade of the Church of the Carmine. Below, left: the nave of the Church, and, right, the frescoed dome.

Facing page: views of the frescoes in the Brancacci Chapel, once more to be seen in their original splendor thanks to recent meticulous restoration.

OTHER CHURCHES

In the pictures, from the top, the **Church of S. Salvatore al Vescovo**, built after 1000, the facade is Romanesque with blind arcades; the **Church of Badia**, built in 978, the portal with a 16th-century lunette is by Benedetto da Rovezzano (1495); and the **Church of S. Carlo dei Lombardi** built between the 14th and 15th century by Benci di Cione, Neri di Fioravante and Simone Talenti. At the bottom, the **Church of S. Salvi**, built as an abbey in 1048, remodeled many times; the **Church of SS. Apostoli**, built in the 11th century with a Romanesque facade, remarkable the interior; and the **Church of S. Gaetano**, whose elevation is the result of the 17th-century restoration by Gherardo Silvani.

Above: the facade of the Church of S. Trinita. Right: the Adoration of the Shepherds by Ghirlandaio

CHURCH OF S. TRINITA

The 11th-century building was rebuilt and enlarged in the 13th and 14th centuries. The linear facade in stone is by Buontalenti (1593). Thanks to the fact that it stands between the Via Tornabuoni and the Ponte S. Trinita, it is one of the best known churches in Florence. Tradition ascribes the project to Andrea Pisano, the result of the remodelling of a Vallombrosan convent that already stood on the site. The simple lean interior houses important works of art such as the Madonna and Saints by Neri di Ricci (1491), the Annunciation by Lorenzo Monaco (1425), and Ghirlandaio's Adoration of the Shepherds (1485). The frescoes in the **Sassetti Chapel** *(1483-1486) are also by Ghirlandaio. The tombs of the Sassetti family are by Giuliano da Sangallo. The second chapel to the left of the high altar (with a triptych by Mariotto di Nardo, 1416) contains the tomb of the Bishop of Fiesole by Luca della Robbia (1454-1456).*

FROM THE SEVENTEENTH CENTURY TO THE TWENTIETH CENTURY

In 1574 Cosimo I left the government in the hands of his son Francesco who reigned till 1587 when he was succeeded by his brother Ferdinando I (1587-1609). The latter continued his father's policy and succeeded in strengthening the grand duchy, maintaining a difficult equilibrium between France and Spain. Signs of decadence became more obvious under the government of these two sons of Cosimo I's and were accellerated in the 17th century. Florence was still a great city, but its territory was small and it could certainly not compete with the great and powerful centralized states. Economically the situation had also changed. Trade and manufacturing were on the decline and, at least up to the end of the 16th century, only banking was still carried out on a European level, but in the end that too declined. The efforts of the grand ducal governments to give new life to business by developing the port of Livorno and the founding of the military order of Saint Stephen for the protection of the Florentine navy from the «barbareschi» were to no avail. On the contrary agriculture grew in importance in Tuscany and in the second half of the 16th century large reclamation projects were undertaken in various parts of the region. In the final decades of the 16th century and in the period around the turn of the century the cultural and artistic life of Florence was clearly nearing the end of the most felicitous period in the history of the city, even though works of relevance were still being produced. Mannerist tendencies crept into architecture as it submitted ever more frequently to caprice and naturalism. This has already been noted in the works of Buontalenti but is more evident in Federico Zuccari (see his *house studio* in the Via Giusti), in the nymphaeums and grottoes with which artists like Ammannati, Giambologna and Tribolo embellished the gardens of the urban and suburban villas, and even in the coats of arms and the scroll ornaments set on the facades of the palaces which more and more frequently were frescoed or decorated with sgraffito.

Ferdinando I was succeeded by the «weak and sickly» Cosimo II (1609-1621) who died leaving the government in the hands of his wife Maria Magdalena of Austria and his mother Christine of Lorraine. In 1628, when the period of the regency came to an end, Ferdinando II mounted the throne and reigned until 1670. Even though he was reputed to be «among the best of the Medici dynasty», he could do nothing to arrest the inexorable decline of Florence and of the Tuscany of the grand dukes. Nor could his successors, Cosimo III (1670-1723) and the last of the Medici dynasty, Gian Gastone, who died without heirs in 1737. Even so, as far as culture was concerned, the city, by now condemned to a provincial role, still displayed a certain vitality which expressed itself in the field of music (melodramma, with the famous «Camerata di Casa Bardi», was born in Florence at the end of the 16th century) and in the phenomenon of the Academies.

From the late 16th century on and throughout the 17th century numerous academies of pure literature came into being. The **Accademia della Crusca** whose principal labor was the compilation of the *Dictionary*, the first edition of which appeared in 1612, was founded in 1582. Of great importance for the sciences was the activity of the **Accademia del Cimento**, founded by Leopoldo de' Medici in 1657 and sustained by his brother, the reigning Ferdinando II. Both were pupils of Galileo, the only man of genius the 17th century produced in the grand duchy.

While at the beginning of the 17th century Tuscany could still be counted as one of the economically most developed regions in the western world, under the last of the grand dukes its features became those of a depressed area. Agriculture became by far the most important activity, while trade and manufacturing occupied a marginal role. A significant example is that the production of woolen cloth, which in Florence in 1560-1580 was of approximately 30,000 lengths, fell to barely 5,000 units around the middle of the 17th century. The basic reason for this economic regression is to be identified in the «sclerosis» of the corporations of the Guilds and therefore in the fact that the products of Tuscan industry were no longer competitive, which made it impossible to keep up exportation, and the drop of exportation resulted in a systematic withdrawal of funds from the sectors of manufacturing and trade which in turn had negative effects on internal demand. All this resulted in a tendency to shift the available resources from the manufacturing and service sectors to agriculture, whence the phenomenon of «ruralization» of the grand duchy.

The decline was reflected in architecture and town planning, and activity in these fields was limited and rarely outstanding. In the majority of cases works of restructuration or modernization were involved, especially in the field of religious architecture. On the whole faith was kept with a Mannerist style inspired by Michelangelo, a sort of «constitutional reluctance to accept the Baroque emphasis». Only Matteo Nigetti seemed to indulge in a 17th-century Roman taste in the church of **San Gaetano**, done together with Gherardo Silvani, and in the **facade** of the church **of Ognissanti**, as well as in the monumental **Chapel of the Princes**, with the «almost imperial magnificence» of its interior. A sumptuous decoration also characterizes the **Corsini Chapel** at the **Carmine** and the **interior** of **Santissima Annunziata**, both works by Pier Francesco Silvani and Ciro Ferri, two artists who also collaborated in the severe opulence of the **Cappella Maggiore** of the church of **Santa Maria Maddalena dei Pazzi**. But on the whole the architects who worked in Florence in the 17th century remained basically aloof from the new Roman style (with the exception of Giovan Battista Foggini in the **Ferroni Chapel** in **Santissima Annunziata**) and continued to work in the wake of the best 16th-century tradition. The architecture of 17th-

Palazzo Antellesi in Piazza S. Croce.

The Villa of Poggio Imperiale.

century Florence fills a niche all its own in the over-all picture of that period. While the Baroque of Roman imprint was triumphant elsewhere, the choice in Florence, perhaps unconsciously, seemed to herald future developments. To define the inspiration shared by most of the works of this period as «protoclassicism» does not in our opinion seem hazarded. These works range from the church of **Santa Margherita dei Ricci** (by Gherardo Silvani, 1640) and **Santa Teresa** (Sigismondo Coccapani, 1628), to the **crypt** of **Santo Stefano al Ponte** (Ferdinando Tacca, 1640-1650); from the **interior** of **San Simone** (Gherardo Silvani, 1630) to the church of **San Frediano in Cestello** (by Cerutti, completed in the dome by Antonio Ferri, 1680-1698), up to the church of **San Firenze**, the main example of the architecture known as «Baroque» in Florence, begun by Gherardo Silvani and Pietro da Cortona in the early years of the 17th century and finished by other masters in the next century.

Civil architecture, both the palaces of the aristocracy and the rare public works, remained singularly faithful to the late Renaissance tradition. Among the latter, mention should be made of the **portico of the hospital of Santa Maria Nuova**, designed by Buontalenti but built and continued in 1611-1618 by Giulio Parigi, the

Left: the Loggia del Grano, and, right, a detail of the fountain at the corner.

Loggia-grain market (executed by Parigi in 1619) and, at the end of the century (1695), the **grain warehouse** (**Granaio**) which Cosimo III had built next to the *church of Cestello* by Giovan Battista Foggini, official architect of the grand duchy. As far as private buildings were concerned, only in **Palazzo Corsini** (1648-1656) did Antonio Ferri and Pier Francesco Silvani yield to Roman taste. Later at the beginning of the 18th century, the same was to hold true for **Palazzo Capponi**, built by the architects Ferdinando Ruggeri and Cecchini, on a project by the Roman Carlo Fontana. But the rest of the patrician dwellings adhered closely to the local idiom as can be seen in the numerous palaces attributed to Gherardo Silvani (**Palazzo Guadagni-Riccardi**, now Strozzi in the Via dell'Oriuolo; **Palazzo San Clemente**, in the Via Gino Capponi; **Palazzo Bartolommei**, in the Via Cavour; **Palazzo Marucelli**, later Fenzi, in the Via San Gallo), as well as **Palazzo degli Antellesi**, in the Piazza Santa Croce, and the **Villa del Poggio Imperiale**, both by Giulio Parigi; the **Palazzo Zacchini-Ricasoli**, in the Via Maggio, etc.

THE EIGHTEENTH CENTURY

After the death of Gian Gastone the great powers in Vienna decided to give Tuscany to Francis I Duke of Lorraine who had been forced to cede his duchy to Stanislas Leszczynski, deposed king of Poland. Husband of heir to the imperial throne, Maria Theresa, Francis limited himself to a solemn visit to Florence in 1739, commemorated in the **arch of triumph** erected opposite Porta San Gallo by the French architect Jean-Nicolas Jadot. The new grand duke soon returned to Vienna from where he preferred to govern through a Regent Council whose members came mostly from Lorraine and from Lombardy. The advent of the house of Lorraine marked the beginning of a recovery for Florence and for Tuscany. From the first provisions on, the policy was one of reform in line with the principles of enlightened absolutism, which were to be further developed under the rule of Peter Leopold. He was the third child of Francis and succeeded his father in 1765. In Florence where he lived and was surrounded by illustrious men such as Pompeo Neri, Angelo Tavanti, Francesco Gianni, he succeeded in his aims of giving new strength to the economic and social life of the grand duchy. Leopold's reforms were directed first of all at agriculture, the basic economic activity of the land, but also concerned industry, communications, commerce and what is at present called «cultural policy». «Cultural policy» concerned Florence in particular for the city had managed to preserve a certain intellectual development from the splendor of the past, and it became the center of the cultural activities of the grand duchy, seat of the new Accademia dei Georgofili, founded to promote a more rational agriculture, of the new Istituto per il Deposito del materiale documentario (the future State Archives), new libraries and scientific institutes as well as numerous theaters. Notable too was the town planning policy launched by Grand Duke Leopold, who reorganized the public services and increased their efficiency. Particular attention was paid to health and instruction: hospitals were created *ex-novo* and those extant were enlarged. Public schools, conservatories and professional chairs of agriculture, law and medicine were instituted. An important aspect of town planning was the creation of new green areas in the city such as the *Parterre* of San Gallo, the avenue of Poggio Imperiale, the field of *San Salvatore al Monte* and numerous other public walks. The park of the grand duke's *Cascine* was opened to the public on special occasions. Moreover, still under Peter Leopold, the Piazza San Marco took on its present features: the new facade of the church was realized by Gioachino Pronti (1780), the *hospital of San Matteo* was remodelled and the «**Palazzina**» **of Livia Malfatti** was built. The «Palazzina» by Bernardo Fallani (1775-1778) is one of the most significant examples of the late Mannerist architecture which was to continue to dominate Florence at the height of the 18th century, as witnessed by the works of other Florentine artists active in those years: Ferdinando Ruggieri, Zanobi Del Rosso, Giuseppe Salvetti, Gaspare Maria Paoletti, Giulio Mannaioni and Giuseppe Ruggeri. The two last named remodelled the **interior** of the church of the **Carmine** after the fire which semi-

destroyed the church in 1771, while between 1772 and 1775 Zanobi Del Rosso finished the complex of **San Firenze**, building the right wing and the central structure, and in 1736 Giuseppe Ruggeri renovated the church of **Santa Felicita**. But in the meanwhile the neoclassic movement began to gain ground among the architects who gravitated around the grand duke's court so that in the final decades of the century Florentine architecture evolved in the direction of a new figurative syntax. The school of Gaspare Maria Paoletti, whom Peter Leopold had named «Maestro di Architettura» in the Accademia di Belle Arti which the grand duke himself had founded, was the formative element for the group of architects-engineers (Giuseppe Del Rosso, Luigi Cambray-Digny, Giuseppe Cacialli, Pasquale Poccianti) who were responsible for most of the neoclassic works to be found in Florence and in Tuscany. Paoletti, who together with G. Manetti attended to the installation of the *Parco delle Cascine* (they designed the **Peacock House**, the **Fount of Narcissus**, the **Pyramid**, etc.), planned and began the building of the **Meridiana** in **Palazzo Pitti**, later finished at the beginning of the 19th century by Poccianti. Between 1764 and 1765, Giuseppe Ruggeri also built the *loggia* of the bodyguard with its neoclassic accents in *Palazzo Pitti*, the first of the two lateral projections (the so-called *rondò*) designed by Ignazio Pellegrini to complete the palace which had already been enlarged in the 17th century by Alfonso Parigi and now was the object of a whole series of manipulations, rearrangement and restructuration.

The modernization of the civil structures was a phenomenon that characterized a good part of the building fabric of the city which changed a great deal between the end of the 18th century and the early decades of the 19th century. This was the period in which the facades of the Florentine houses were plastered (at times chiseling into the medieval rustication in *pietra forte*),

The large round pond in the Park of the Cascine.

The Palazzina of Livia Malfatti.

round-arched openings were replaced by classicizing windows with lintels or by edicule windows with triangular pediments, the interiors (above all the staircases) were modified and the principal facades were embellished with string courses in *pietra serena* and only slightly projecting cornice moldings. In 1792, during restoration of the *Palazzo Vecchio*, even the tower was plastered!

THE NINETEENTH CENTURY

Called to the imperial crown, in 1790 Peter Leopold left the grand duchy to his second son, Ferdinand, whose reign was interrupted by fifteen years of French occupation (from 1799 to 1814). First Napoleon constituted a kingdom of Etruria, which he gave to the Bourbons of Parma (treaty of Lunéville), then he annexed Tuscany, divided into three departments, to the French empire. Florence, which had been capital of the kingdom of Etruria from 1801 to 1807, from 1807 to 1814 became simply the chief town of the department of the Arno. If, as Y. Renouard justly affirms, the enlightened government of the house of Lorraine had left «few things for the ideas and the men of the French Revolution to change when they entered Tuscany», it is also true that during the fifteen years of French occupation a series of improvements regarding the organization of civil life were carried out in Florence and in the grand duchy as a whole. These achievements took the form of public works, administrative reforms and interventions on a territorial and town-planning level. As far as Florence is concerned mention must be made specifically of the urban transformation which resulted from the incorporation of the belongings of the religious orders into public property. Indeed, the suppres-

sion of the orders in 1808 put vast urban areas and buildings at the disposal of the city and they were subsequently adapted to new uses, mostly of a public nature. The most important examples of architecture of those years include works by Giuseppe Del Rosso, who also designed the grandiose projects (never realized) for urban reorganization. Fruit of Del Rosso's activity is also the so-called *Deposito di Mendicità* (later **Pia Casa dei Lavoro**), built in 1808 on the order of the French government after the Convents of Monticelli and Montedomini had been suppressed, as well as the **Liceo Regio** in the Borgo Pinti (1812-1813).

The restoration of the house of Lorraine in 1814 did not annul most of the improvements the French had initiated, despite the fact that Ferdinand III eliminated all forms of civic liberty. The new ideas and ferments introduced by the French and assimilated by public opinion gradually resulted in the detachment of the population, above all the more cultured strata, from the Lorraine dynasty which was too closely tied to Austria and the Reaction. And this was what happened notwithstanding the reforms that were fostered (such as the one which led to the compilation of the Catasto Geometrico Particellare Toscano or Tuscan Land Register) and the excellent administration of the governments of the grand duchy, especially under Leopold II (1824-1859), which did its best to modernize Tuscany, encouraging industrial development. Under the last grand duke the various interventions which modified the city's set-up were also effectuated. Their scope was that of rendering certain traffic routes more efficient and of «regularizing» certain urban structures. The Via Larga was thus extended to create what is now the Via Cavour (then called Via San Leopoldo), parallel to the pre-existing Via San Gallo; the Via Salvestrina and the Via Apollonia (later XXVII Aprile) were opened up, with the scope of developing the area around the Piazza Maria Antonia (now Piazza Indipendenza); the Via Calzaioli was broadened with the loss however of significant medieval building evidence; two iron bridges over the Arno were built, designed by the Séguin brothers, French engineers and owners of the firm of the same name: San Ferdinando, upstream from the city, and San Leopoldo, downstream, in correspondence to where the bridges, respectively, of San Niccolò and della Vittoria were to rise; the railroad station «Maria Antonia» was built behind the apse of *Santa Maria Novella*. This was the second railway station of Florence for in precedence with the laying of the first stretch of railroad of the grand duchy (the Florence-Pisa line), another station had been built outside Porta al Prato for the sake of prudence.

Among the most important buildings of the time mention must be made of various interesting neoclassic constructions, works of Gaetano Baccani (the **Palazzo dei Principi Borghese** in the Via Ghibellina, the **Palazzo dei Canonici** in the Piazza del Duomo, the **Palazzo Durazzo-Stacchini** in the Via Torta, by Giuseppe Martelli, the **Terrazzino Reale sul Prato**, by Luigi Cambray-Digny (from the loggia, which is now a blind arcade, the rulers took part in the horse race or *corsa dei barberi*), the interventions of Poccianti in the *Palazzo Pitti* and in the *Laurentian Library*, to the **Camposanto della Misericordia** and the enormous building (which then became the seat of the Teatro Pagliano and then, what is now **Teatro Verdi**) which were erected on the area of the old *prisons of the Stinche*, demolished in 1838. But in the very years when these restrained neoclassical buildings were being built, the first examples of Neo-Gothic architecture appeared, including the **bell tower of Santa Croce** and the **Torrino** in the garden of the **Palazzo Serristori** in the Via dei Serragli, both by Baccani, and the curious **Palazzina sul Prato** the sculptor Ignazio Villa built for himself.

In the meantime the city, as a consequence of the modest but not irrelevant process of industrialization, as well as the general economic growth, for the first time in five centuries witnessed a considerable increase in population. In fifteen years (1844 to 1859) it rose from 81,000 to 113,000 inhabitants. The urban fabric which developed as a result was however still contained within the 14th-century city walls, for the new constructions occupied the internal gardens and above all the large areas right next to the walls used for vegetable gardens. In addition to the «spontaneous» interventions, the growth of the city was also regulated by a real town planning program which provided for (and realized) the first residential quarters. The area once occupied by the «farms of Barbano» around the new Piazza Maria Antonia (the first 19th-century square in Florence) was to see the creation, between 1844 and 1855, of the district then called *di Barbano* which was reserved primarily for the middle classes (artisans, clerks). Likewise in correspondence to that part of the *Parco delle Cascine* which originally expanded as far as the peach orchard of Santa Rosa, the quarter of the same name, reserved for the more well to do classes, rose between 1850 and 1855. On this occasion the **Lungarno Nuovo** (now Lungarno Amerigo Vespucci) was built and lined with buildings in neoclassic taste erected by the principal exponents of the city's middle class. The creation of the first residential quarters introduced a «functional and social» selection which accentuated the subdivision of the city into zones that became characterized by their functions. Indeed in the middle of the 19th century the urban fabric already contained areas that were clearly defined by the great number of buildings whose function was prevalently public. For example the area between the Via San Gallo, the Borgo Pinti and the line of the next to last belt of city walls contained the greater part of the hospitals and charity buildings, the schools, the government offices, etc. In the zone of Santa Croce there were army barracks, prisons and the *Deposito di Mendicità* of the *Pia Casa del Lavoro*. The Oltrarno, thanks to the presence of the Palazzo Pitti, contained all those services and facilities which were related to the grand ducal court. And so on.

In the years of the Lorraine restoration Florence also became an extremely active cultural center, perhaps the most important in Italy. The presence of foreigners and travelers who visited the city in ever increasing numbers, often choosing to stay, was particularly stimulating. The activities of the *Gabinetto* for reading and discussion founded in 1819 by Giampietro Vieussieux, the journal «*L'Antologia*», the Archivio Storico Italiano were the principal expressions of the new liberal and national ideas that spread among the intellectuals and the deep-seated aspiration for independence in the framework of a united Italy.

After the movements of 1848, the flight of Leopold II and his return the next year, escorted by Austrian troops, extraneated public opinion even more from the grand duke. On April 22, 1859, taking advantage of the war that Napoleon and the king of Sardinia were waging against Austria and with a practically unanimous desire on the part of the population, Leopold was forced, this time definitively, to abandon the grand duchy. A provvisory government was set up in Florence. Under the guidance of Bettino Ricasoli the city decided, with the plebiscite of 1860, to be annexed to the Kingdom of Sardinia and then to the new Kingdom of Italy. The fact that Florence consciously relinquished its autonomy in favor of the realization of a large common fatherland increased the city's moral authority and in 1865 it was proclaimed capital of Italy, partly out of political and geographic reasons, but also because of its great historical and cultural traditions.

The transferral of the Court, of the Ministries and the offices of the Kingdom of Italy, and above all of the circa 20,000 people who constituted its personnel, created serious problems for the small regional capital which is what Florence had basically been up until then. Unlike Torino, a more modern city whose city plan had been in great part dictated by the enlargements of the 17th and 18th centuries, creating a clear and ordered urban fabric, Florence was a city that was still basically as it had been in the 16th century. It was fairly easy to find place for the Court, the Ministers, the Parliament, etc., utilizing the principal palaces of the city, as well as religious buildings which had become available when ecclesiastical property was expropriated. But this was not the case for the 20,000 people representing the lists of the new government. The problem of lodgings and of controlling rents made itself urgently felt. Those who suffered most were the lower classes and particularly the poorest families. The construction of dwellings in the new residential areas realized in the sixties and seventies (districts of Maglio and Mattonaia), swiftly as they were raised, only partly fulfilled the demand for lodgings. In addition the new buildings were appanage of the middle classes and the lower working classes often had to content themselves with living in temporary structures in iron and wood, set up by the City at Porta alla Croce, the Pignone and outside Porta San Frediano. The urban growth which resulted from this further increase in the population (150,000 inhabitants in 1865) led to the spread of the city outside the 14th-century walls. The epansion would have been chaotic had it not been governed by a city plan which a valiant architect, Giuseppe Poggi, was called upon to provide. Not everything planned by Poggi was realized (the initial plans were successively reelaborated in a second version) however the principal interventions rapidly carried out were sufficient to set the development of Florence off in the right direction in the years that were to follow and up almost to World War I. The concept upon which the plan was based was that of creating an urban expansion along the lines of an «undifferentiated and purely residential checkerboard» which would lead to the distinction, previously inexistent, of a city center and various peripherical areas. The need to find wide open areas and provide an outlet for the growth led to the demolition of the walls on this side of the Arno and the realization in their place of broad tree-shaded avenues punctuated by symmetrical squares built in correspondence to the old city gates, almost all of which were preserved (except Porta a Pinti). The **avenues**, which echoed Haussmann's projects in Paris and the *ring* of Vienna, were not, in Poggi's plan, to be interrupted but were to have continued beyond Porta Romana, as far as the Cascine thus making a ring all around the city.

The group of copies with David at the top in the center of Piazzale Michelangelo.

The **Piazzale Michelangelo** and the walk of the Viale dei Colli which leads there may represent the most celebrated of Poggi's realizations, and there is no doubt but that the installation of a «belvedere» above the city corresponded in full to the tastes of 19th-century culture. The creation of the piazzale, the intrusion of the neo-Renaissance *building of the Loggia Caffè* and the construction of the futile and somewhat pompous staircase that led to the Romanesque basilica were certainly no improvement as far as the two churches of *San Salvatore* and *San Miniato* which crown the hill were concerned. Internally the city broadened and unified its main streets, in the wake of a tendency that came to the fore in the last decades of the grand ducal government when the Via Cerretani and the Via Panzani were broadened (to facilitate communications between the Piazza del Duomo and the railroad station) as well as the Via Strozzi, the Via Tornabuoni and the last stretch of the Via dell'Oriuolo. With an eye to improving the aspect of the city it was decided to complete the old monuments: the *cathedral* and *Santa Croce* thus both obtained their facades. Apart from the debatable results (especially for the cathedral) two of those «great mute walls which loom over the major piazzas of Florence and which

corresponded, deep down, as no drawing could ever or would ever have done, to the Florentine spirit» (G. Fanelli) had now disappeared.

With the taking of Rome and the transferral of the capital to the banks of the Tiber (July 1, 1871), urban expansion came to a halt. The population shrank (in three years the number dropped by as many as 28,000) and the entire productivity of the city was negatively influenced by the recession which followed the years of the economic boom. Despite this, the municipal city council with its mayor Ubaldino Peruzzi decided to continue the work that had been begun and even to initiate other projects of restructurization as outlined in Poggi's plan. This led to the opening up of the *lung-arni*, and the consequent demolition of the characteristic houses on wooden corbels which in many places still faced on the Arno, the destruction of the complex of the old mills and the mint and the affirmation of a new relationship between the city and the river. Other streets were widened or opened *ex-novo* and, in the interests of facilitating traffic and communications the restoration of the old center was decided, justifying the operation on hygienic grounds. With the demolition of 1885 what was to be remembered as the greatest town-planning error of the century was begun. Rare frag-

Panorama of Florence from the Belvedere in the Piazzale Michelangelo: outstanding landmarks from left to right are the Ponte Vecchio, Palazzo Vecchio, the Duomo and Santa Croce.

ments of the pre-existing urban fabric were spared, a choice dictated by the concept of «monument», uprooted from the surrounding urban context. The buildings saved were few. The churches of *Sant'Andrea* and *San Pier Buonconsiglio* were destroyed as well as *San Tommaso* and *Santa Maria in Campidoglio*. The *headquarters of the Arte degli Albergatori* and the *Arte dei Rigattieri* disappeared together with the *towerhouses of the Almieri* and the *Caponsacchi*. Only occasionally were architectural or decorative elements of other buildings saved and deposited in museums. At times a whole piece would be disassembled and recomposed elsewhere, such as the *tabernacle of Santa Maria della Tromba* which was set up on the corner of the *palace of the Arte della Lana*. After having been disemboweled, the streets which tended to follow the orthogonal Roman plan but whose course had been slightly modified in the Middle Ages were straightened out and

lined with new anonymous buildings which corresponded to the needs of bourgeois decorum and «*signorilità*». Lastly the Piazza del Mercato Vecchio was enlarged with **porticoes**. At the top of the awkward arch the words «L'antico centro della città da secolare squallore a vita nuova restituita» (The ancient city center restored to new life after centuries of squalor) sounds unconsciously ironic.

The seventies saw the construction of new and more functional markets, fulfilling a need that had arisen with the elimination of the Mercato Vecchio, already planned in the years Florence was capital. The **central market of San Lorenzo**, built in iron on plans by Giuseppe Mengoni (who had also designed the Gallery in Milan) and inaugurated in 1874, led to the demolition of still another part of the medieval urban fabric. On the other hand room for the **district market of Sant'Ambrogio**, realized in 1873, also in iron, was found

on the grounds of the vast vegetable gardens which stretched beyond the church of *Santa Croce*. Another district market place, later done away with, was inaugurated in 1875 in San Frediano in the Piazza dei Nerli. The demolition which accompanied the restructuration and reorganization of the old city center and the adjacent areas, was, like all the other interventions, a result of building speculation. Its social cost was enormous and it initiated a process of transformation, turning the center into a sort of small «city», the seat of management activities (banks, insurance companies, professional studios, etc.). The humbler levels of society - originally the majority - were pushed out towards the popular districts of Santa Croce and San Frediano, increasing the population density in an area that was already densely populated. The urban structures degraded as a result of superstructures and the elimination of the residual green areas (vegetable and

flower gardens) and the courtyards. But the more prosperous part of the population abandoned the center and settled down into the «upper quarters» of some of the peripherical zones, that is in the areas beyond or on the boulevards, where the new urban fabric took shape along the lines of bourgeois conformity and respectability.

THE TWENTIETH CENTURY

The industrial development (relatively speaking) of Italy in the 1890s and the early twentieth century also involved Florence and determined the rapid growth of the population which increased by 50,000 in 25 years. No over-all plan regulated the sites for the factories and they sprang up haphazardly along the natural sites

View of the Piazza del Mercato Vecchio, completely rebuilt in the 19th century, in a painting by Telemaco Signorini, in the Museo di Firenze Com'era.

of agglomeration on the antique *vie regie*, the principal roads that left the city, and the railroad. The area north of the railroad (freight station of Campo di Marte) and of Rifredi (roads that communicated with the busy centers in the Florentine basin) were the first industrial zones.

The rise in population obviously stimulated building activity, above all with regards to the edification of popular housing. More than 36,000 rooms were built between 1905 and 1913, in great part utilizing the areas along the edge of the walled city. Characteristic for the period were the two-story buildings which still flank some of the streets on the other side of the boulevards that run around the city, outside the Porta San Frediano and in the quarters of San Jacopino and San Salvi. The Cure and San Gervasio-Campo di Marte were prevalently reserved for the middle and prosperous upper middle-class dwellings. A great many *villini* or small villas, the typical bourgeois dwellings of the late 19th-early 20th century, were built especially (but not exclusively) in these areas. They are often interesting examples of Art Nouveau (see the *villini* built by Giovanni Michelazzi) or neo-Renaissance styles (see the **Villa Favard** by Giuseppe Poggi and many of the buildings which line the avenues, the *lungarni*, Piazza d'Azeglio, etc.).

In the absence of a town plan to regulate the growth of the city, as Poggi had tried to do, at least approximately, in the period when Florence was the capital, the intense building activity led to a creeping expansion of the urban nucleus. A new town plan was not prepared until 1915 and even then it did not become effective till 1924. Its scope was that of rationalizing the extant situation through interventions in the sectors, and of increasing the number of streets in the outlying areas, invading the unoccupied level areas as far as the foothills. The plan also called for the reclamation of some of the residential areas of the «old» city, but fortunately these projects were only carried out in part in the quarter of Santa Croce where a few city blocks were torn down in 1936.

During the Fascist period popular housing resulted in various residential complexes built in areas that were at the time peripherical but which were later swallowed up by the expanding city. But attention was turned primarily to the demagogic realization of monumental constructions which represented the regime. Some rather insignificant structures (such as the *Casa del Balilla* in the Piazza Beccaria, recently torn down) went up but there were also outstanding examples of architecture such as the **City Stadium** by Pier Luigi Nervi (1932) and the new **Railroad Station** (1935) by a group of architects under the direction of Giovani Michelucci. During the Fascist dictatorship, work continued on the **Biblioteca Nazionale Centrale**, an enormous building in questionable style defined by Emilio Cecchi as a «balcanizing Kursaal» built around one of Brunelleschi's loveliest cloisters - a heavy-handed intervention in the city's urban fabric.

During World War II Florence was quite heavily damaged and its artistic heritage was gravely impaired. The destruction was at its worst when the city found itself in the line of fire. The retreating Germans blew up all the bridges except the *Ponte Vecchio* which was blocked with the rubble from the surrounding houses, any number of which in a vast radius had literally been razed to the ground. With the *Ponte a Santa Trinita* (later rebuilt «as it was and where it was») some of the most typical quarters of medieval Florence were destroyed.

From the fifties on, the city, which in the years preceding World War II had already exceeded 300,000 inhabitants, became involved in the most impressive population boom in its long history. In 20 years the population rose from 374,000 in 1951 to 457,000 in 1971. The zones surrounding the city were literally invaded by an unbelievably chaotic expansion of the building fabric, the result of uncontrolled speculation. Only recently the approval of an overall town plan (Sept. 5, 1966) has provided for real urban planning in the framework of a profound renewal of the way in which the territory is managed.

THE ARNO, THE STREETS, THE PIAZZAS

PONTE VECCHO AND BRIDGES OF FLORENCE

The oldest bridge in the city. **Vasari's Corridor** crosses it above the shops of the craftsmen. The ten bridges across the Arno. **Ponte S. Trinita**, with scroll ornaments and statues.

PIAZZA S. TRINITA

An asymmetrical square with the **Column of Justice** at the center.

PIAZZA DELLA REPUBBLICA

In 1887 ancient quarters and the Hebrew ghetto were demolished to make way for this piazza in the heart of the city, on the site of the ancient Roman Forum. In the background, the large **Arch**.

PALAZZO STROZZI

Renaissance palace by Benedetto da Maiano. Inside: the **Courtyard** and the **loggia**.

PALAZZO MEDICI-RICCARDI (Via Cavour)

The residence of the Medici family. Inside: the **Courtyard**, the **Chapel** frescoed by Benozzo Gozzoli and the **Room** with frescoes by Luca Giordano.

SYNAGOGUE (Via Farini)

Nineteenth-century Hebrew temple. Near it a complex of buildings to be used by the Hebrew community and the rooms of the **Museo Israelitico**.

CITY GATES OF FLORENCE

In the Oltrarno area they are still attached to the city walls. On this side of the river: the **Porta alla Croce** in Piazza Beccaria, the **Porta al Prato** and the **Porta S. Gallo**, at the center of squares along the circumvallation boulevards.

Above: Ponte Vecchio on the downstream side of the Arno. Left: the Bust of Cellini in the middle of the bridge. Facing page, above: the upstream side of the bridge and, below, a detail of some of the workshops on the bridge and the arches which support Vasari's Corridor.

BRIDGES OF FLORENCE AND THE PONTE VECCHIO
Currently there are ten Florentine bridges, but until 1957 there were six, modified in the course of the centuries and all, except the Ponte Vecchio, rebuilt after their destruction in 1944 by mines. The **Ponte Vecchio** is the oldest bridge in the city, not only because it is the only one which survived, but also because it stands on the site of at least three precedent bridges: one in Roman times, the one that was ruined in 1117, and the one destroyed when the Arno flooded in 1333. The bridge so greatly admired now was built by Neri di Fioravante (1345), a solid but elegant structure with three arches. It is characterized by the small houses that line both sides of the bridge. In the 14th century these rows of buildings had a much more regular appearance but as time went by various changes and additions led to their current picturesque variety. At about the center of the span over the river, the buildings are interrupted by a widening of the roadway, thus furnishing a fine view of the Arno and the other bridges.
Vasari's Corridor passes along over the bridge, above the buildings. It allowed Cosimo I to reach Palazzo Pitti from Palazzo Vecchio without running any risks. Ever since the 16th century the shops on the bridge have been the laboratory-shops of goldsmiths (previously some of them were butcher shops).
The second Florentine bridge was the **Ponte Nuovo** or

Ponte alla Carraia (1220), which served for the heavy traffic of the time. It was also reconstructed after the floods of 1274 and 1333, and then once more after it fell in 1944. The third bridge was the *Ponte alle Grazie* (1237), so-called because of a chapel dedicated to the Madonna delle Grazie. What we see now is post-war. The fourth bridge is the *Ponte S. Trinita*, a masterpiece by Ammannati (1567-70); Michelangelo supervised the project. It replaced previous bridges (the earliest dated to 1257) which had been carried away by the floods. At the beginning and end of the bridge are the statues of the Four Seasons (set there in 1608). The present bridge is the result of a reconstruction carried out « as it was and where it was » in the 1950s, after it had been destroyed in the war. The other two bridges date to the 19th century — the one of *S. Niccolò* and the one at the Cascine (which was originally a suspended bridge), rebaptized in 1928 *Ponte alla Vittoria*. The *Ponte Vespucci* was inaugurated in 1957. It is the first modern bridge and the seventh in the series. In 1969 *Ponte Giovanni da Verrazzano* was added and, recently, the *Viaduct of the Indian*, beyond the Cascine, and the one of *Varlungo*.

THE MANNELLI TOWER
The Mannelli tower belonged to the Manelli family, in origin Ghibelline, that later split into two factions: Guelph and Ghibelline. Luckily this building was saved from demolition. Vasari's Corridor, the building of which was ordered by Cosimo I, was to have passed through it. After the protests of Mannelli, the Grand Duke left the building intact. We can still see it on the Oltrarno side of the Ponte Vecchio.

Left: the Mannelli Tower. Below: Ponte Vecchio and its shops. Facing page, above: Ponte S. Trinita and Ponte Vecchio; below: Ponte S. Trinita on the upstream side.

BRIDGE AND CHURCH OF SANTA TRINITA

The **Bridge of Santa Trinita** is adorned with the statues of Spring and Summer on the northern side towards the center (opposite; left, below). Walking past **Ferroni Palace** (opposite, above) we reach **Piazza Santa Trinita** (opposite; right, below), adorned in the center with the **Column of Justice**, a Roman shaft originally from the Baths of Caracalla with the statue of Justice on the top.

PIAZZA DELLA REPUBBLICA

What was once the ancient Roman forum where the cardo and the decumanus crossed, was the lively center of the Mercato Vecchio (Old Market) in medieval times. It acquired its present aspect, anonymous and in Piedmontese style, when the center of Florence was torn down in 1887, so lamentable in many ways. The old towers and houses, the historical Hebrew ghetto, churches, shops and open-air markets gave way to the palaces, cafés, and the enormous arcade that leads to the Via Strozzi, dedicated together with the square to Vittorio Emanuele II.

PALAZZO STROZZI

This typical example of a Renaissance palace was designed by Benedetto da Maiano in 1489 (work continued under various superintendents until 1538). The broad portal with a rusticated arch and the rectangular windows are set into the lower part in pietra forte. The upper part, attributed to il Cronaca, is articulated by two denticular cornices of classic taste, while a large cornice crowns the building. The windows are two-light openings.

Right: Palazzo Strozzi. Below: Piazza della Repubblica.

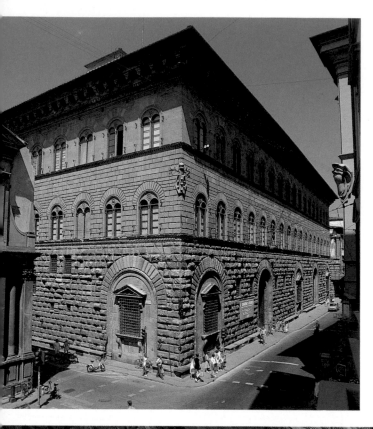

PALAZZO MEDICI-RICCARDI

This is the palace Cosimo the Elder had built for himself and his family. The work of Michelozzo (1444-1464), it is a model of the Renaissance upper-class dwelling. In 1517 the open loggia on the ground floor was walled up and the pedimented windows attributed to Michelangelo were added. In 1655 it was acquired by the Riccardi family who added on to the facade and the whole building, thus altering the original aspect. Outside, as the facade rises, the pronounced rustication of the ground floor passes to a smooth rustication to finely fitted flat slabs on the uppermost floor. The two-light windows have a small column topped by a roundel. A cornice on corbels, classical in style, runs along the top of the building. The palace, which once belonged to Lorenzo the Magnificent and is now the seat of the Prefecture, also contains the famous frescoes by Benozzo Gozzoli of the Arrival of the Magi in Bethlehem in its **Chapel** *(also by Michelozzo). Painted in 1459-60, the fresco portrays the personages present at the Council of Florence in 1439 (recognizable are John VII, Lorenzo, Piero the Gouty with his daughters, Galeazzo Maria Sforza, Sigismondo Malatesta, as well as Benozzo himself and his master, Fra Angelico). Of particular note too is the* **Courtyard** *of the palace, with the porticoes set under a tier of two-light openings and a loggia, decorated with 15th-century graffiti by Maso di Bartolomeo and medallions by Bertoldo.*

Facing page, above, left: Palazzo Medici Riccardi; right: the Room of Luca Giordano. Below and on this page, details of the Chapel in the Palazzo with frescoes by Benozzo Gozzoli depicting the Arrival of the Magi in Bethlehem.

SYNAGOGUE
The Israelite Temple, in an eastern Byzantine style, was designed by the architects Falcini, Treves, Micheli and Cioni (1874). When the large dome was finally covered with copper, it was inaugurated in October of 1882. The construction is interesting both for the elegant frescoes and mosaics which decorate it inside and out, and for its historical and cultural meaning. It is the symbol of the liberation from the ghetto.

CITY GATES OF FLORENCE
Of the many city gates in the 14th-century circuit of walls only eight survived the havoc wreaked by the architect Poggi in 1865. These include the **Porta alla Croce**, **al Prato** and **a San Gallo** on this side of the Arno and **Porta Romana**, **San Frediano**, **San Giorgio**, **San Miniato** and **San Niccolò** (with their walls) on the far side of the river. Missing is the ninth of the principal gates, the Porta a Faenza, as well as the seven minor gates. Porta Romana (1326) merits particular attention for its imposing aspect, and the Porta S. Giorgio (1260) which belonged to the second circle.

This page: the Synagogue, exterior and interior. Facing page, left: Porta di S. Niccolò; right, top to bottom: Porta alla Croce, Romana and S. Giorgio.

MUSEUMS AND GALLERIES

The «condensation» and the «storage» of culture are, as Mumford says «among the main functions of the city and the degree to which it carries out these functions deter mines in part its importance and worth, while the other municipal functions, essential as they may be, are above all accessory and preparatory». The prime role Florence has played in the formative process of modern culture in the city, is the reason why museums and cultural institutions abound in Florence where they contribute to the transmission of human experience and memory, joining the past to the present and the future.

It is common knowledge that the museums of Florence harbor above all (though not exclusively) expressions of artistic culture, of the glorious traditions in the fields of sculpture and painting which belong to the city, cradle of the Renaissance. The **Uffizi** in particular is the principle picture gallery in Italy and one of the most important collections of art in the world. Founded in 1581 by Francesco I de' Medici, as a means of utilizing the upper gallery of the great palace for Magistrates built for Cosimo I by Vasari, the picture gallery has a history four hundred years old. The early *Uffizi* also included the *Tribune*, designed by Buontalenti, some of the small adjacent rooms and the other wing of the Gallery, once occupied by art workshops. In them Francesco I collected a great number of art objects, such as paintings and bronzes, miniatures and enamels, ivories and gems, curiosities and antique medals. With Ferdinando I, famous for his many art acquisitions, the Gallery was considerably enlarged and was enriched with the rooms of the Armory and those for mathematical instruments as well as workshops for the most varied arts. Then in 1631, thanks to the inheritance of Francesco Maria della Rovere, an ancestor of Vittoria, Ferdinando II's wife, numerous works by Raphael and Titian arrived from Urbino. The heredity of Cardinal Leopoldo de' Medici, which fell to his nephew Cosimo II, was even larger and consisted of a choice collection of fine gems and medallions, as well as the famous collections of drawings and self-portraits. When Gian Gastone, the last of the Medicis, died, his sister Anna Maria Lodovica, widow of the Palatine Elector, who was the family heir, managed to persuade the house of Lorraine to leave the art collections in Florence and let them become the object of «common and free enjoyment». The new dynasties continued the work of the Medici. Peter Leopold for example had the Gallery rearranged and enlarged, and created the present staircase with the vestibule and the neoclassic *Sala* in which the famous Niobe, which he had had brought from Rome, was exhibited. Around the end of the 18th century the *Uffizi* was rearranged. At that time many collections were divided and trans-

ferred to other museums permitting the gallery to specialize in painting. In the 19th century further transferrals took place because the art objects were too crowded. For example plans were made between 1830 and 1865 to move the archaeological collections elsewhere. The enlargement of the Gallery was one of the principal problems faced by the great art collection as early as the 19th century, especially after the addition of the picture collection from the *Arcispedale di Santa Maria Nuova* acquired in 1872. Recently *Vasari's Corridor*, which crosses the Arno and joins the *Uffizi* with *Pitti Palace*, has been opened so that at least a part of the Gallery's wealth can be exhibited. In the future, when Vasari's whole building will be available and when the entrance is reorganized, the *Uffizi* should finally find enough room to gather together and exhibit the entire collection.

At present the Gallery, visited annually by more than a million people, furnishes a complete picture of Florentine painting including some of the finest and most significant works, as well as conspicuous groups of paintings by other Italian schools (especially the Venetian school), a valuable core of Flemish paintings and the famous collection of self-portraits (unique in the world).

Numerous pieces of antique sculpture, some of which of high quality, complete the Gallery.

Among 13th-century painting attention should be called to a *Maestà* by Cimabue (13th cent.) formerly on the high altar of the Florentine church of *Santa Trinita*, datable around 1280, and the so-called *Rucellai Madonna* by Duccio di Buoninsegna, which owes its name to the fact that for centuries it was to be seen in the chapel dedicated to the Rucellai family in the Florentine basilica of Santa Maria Novella. Outstanding among the works of the early 14th century are Giotto's *Maestà* (*Madonna Enthroned with Saints*) and an *Annunciation* by Simone Martini. Dating to about 1316 and formerly in the church of Ognissanti, Giotto's Madonna sits full square on her throne, surrounded by a small crowd of angels and saints: «the images are synthetic, strong and severe, but already charged with a clearly human feeling» (L. Berti). Signed and dated 1333, the *Annunciation* by the Sienese painter Simone Martini came to the Uffizi from the cathedral of Siena: «suggestive in the immateriality of the images, in the undulating rhythm which accompanies the gestures, in the refined elegance of the decorative details, it represents one of the high points in Sienese painting.»

The two large triptychs, one by Lorenzo Monaco (*Coronation of the Virgin*) and the other by Gentile da Fabriano (*Adoration of the Magi*), stand out among the works of painters who were active at the end of the 14th and the early 15th century. They are followed by the series of masterpieces of Renaissance art, including works by Fra' Giovanni Angelico, Masaccio, Masolino, Filippo Lippi, Piero della Francesca, Paolo Uccello, Antonio and Piero del Pollaiolo, Botticelli, Mantegna, Pietro Perugino, Luca Signorelli, Domenico Veneziano, Verrocchio, Leonardo, Michelangelo, etc. Piero della Francesca's *Portraits of the Dukes of Urbino, Federico and Battista*, two small panels with the allegorical triumphs of the ducal pair on the back, are famous. In the portrait of Federico, the Duke, in perfect profile, dominates his lands in the background, «immersed in a transparent atmosphere» which contrasts with the solidity of the portrait bust.

The stupendous *Battle of San Romano* by Paolo Uccello together with two other episodes (now, respectively, in the Louvre and in the National Gallery of London) formed a cycle which decorated a room in the Medici palace in the Via Larga. Even in its poetic transfiguration of the subject, the painting admirably reflects the violence and harshness of the encounter, «the pretext for bold foreshortenings and the play of volumetric forms». The Uffizi owns the work by Domenico Veneziano which is basic to an understanding of the artist - the altarpiece painted for the church of Santa Lucia dei Magnoli, representing the *Madonna and Child with Saints*. The colors of the clearly delineated architecture which scans the space and inscribes the three-dimensional figures are intensely luminous. Among Fra Filippo Lippi's works mention must be made at least of the famous *Madonna and Child* painted around 1464 in which the painter attains expressions that are «lyrically romantic in the lovely profile of the Virgin, and in the landscape in the background». To be noted is Antonio del Pollaiolo's small painting of *Hercules and Antaeus*, rediscovered together with its pendant *Hercules and the Hydra*, in 1963 in America. The nervous tense line organizes and articulates the forms of the two struggling figures, transferring an acute sense of drama to the image.

Sandro Botticelli's works are all exhibited in a new room, inaugurated in 1978 and organized on the basis of exhaustive museological studies. «Heir to the functional line of Pollaiolo»,Botticelli «transforms Antonio's spasmodic tension into an almost musical rhythm which will find its highest expression in the large mythological scenes of his maturity» (*Primavera* and the *Birth of Venus*) in which the artist reflects those literary and philosophic myths which exalt man's intelligence and his perfection». (M. Lenzini).

The *Annunciation* which modern critics attribute to the young Leonardo comes from the church of the convent of San Bartolomeo di Monteoliveto. The poetic and pictorial level of the painting cannot but confirm this attribution.

The great Michelangelo is represented in the Uffizi by the famous tondo of the *Holy Family*, painted for the wedding of Agnolo Doni and Maddalena Strozzi. The Madonna seated on the ground and reaching for the Child handed to her from behind by St. Joseph, is bound to the other figures in a chain which forms an «energetic plastic core of strident colors» (L. Berti). Two fine late 14th-century paintings by Hugo van der Goes (the Portinari altarpiece or *Adoration of the Shepherds*) and by Rogier van der Weyden (the *Deposition*) belong to the group of Flemish paintings. They strongly influenced some of the Florentine artists of the time (notably Domenico Ghirlandaio and Filippino Lippi) with their analytic penchant in the landscape and the accentuated characterization of the features.

The major personalities of high Renaissance painting are also represented in the Uffizi: from Andrea del Sarto to Pontormo, from Titian to Parmigianino, from Bronzino to Correggio, from Giovanni Bellini to Raphael, from Giorgione to Albrecht Dürer, to Caravaggio.

Works by Raphael include the young *Self-portrait*, the famous *Madonna of the Goldfinch* and the *Portrait of Leo X with the Cardinals Giulio de' Medici and Luigi de' Rossi*, in all of which the «gentile grace» of Umbria and the artist's first teacher, Perugino, fuse with the art of Leonardo.

The greatest Venetian painter of the second half of the 15th century, Giovanni Bellini, is represented by a *Sacra Allegoria* whose meaning is obscure, in which an indefinable almost metaphysical atmosphere prevails, in an enchanted moment of calm. The Uffizi owns *Solomon's Judgement*, a youthful work by another great Venetian, Giorgione, while there are two paintings by Titian, the leading figure in the Venetian Cinquecento: the *Flora* and the so-called *Urbino Venus*. The latter is a work of his maturity, painted in 1538 for Guidobaldo da Montefeltro. It passed to the Medici in the 17th century with the Della Rovere inheritance. The harmoniously composed forms of the woman are illuminated by a warm light which predominates in the color tonalities throughout the painting.

Found in 1916-17 in the storerooms of the Uffizi, the *Adolescent Bacchus* is one of the works of the very young Caravaggio where «the realistic reduction enhances the image, equal in its naturalness to the fruit and the grape leaves» (L. Berti).

Mention at least among the other works by 16th-century painters should be made of: the *Adoration of the Child* by Antonio Allegri, known as Correggio; the *Portrait of Eleonora of Toledo*, by Bronzino; the so-called *Madonna of the Long Neck*, by Parmigianino; the *Adoration of the Magi*, by Albrecht Dürer; the *Madonna of the Harpies*, by Andrea del Sarto.

Palazzo Pitti, which was the palatial residence of three of the families who most greatly influenced the history of Florence and of Italy, contains numerous works by Italian and foreign masters of the 15th to the 18th century, including many masterpieces of the principal schools of Italian painting (Florentine, Venetian, Emilian, Roman, Neapolitan) and from abroad (Flemish and Spanish schools). What is known as the **Galleria Palatina** is in the tradition of the princely galleries arranged along the lines of ornamental rather than scientific criterion. The value of the paintings is coupled with the magnificence of the decoration, the furniture and the numerous objects.

Begun by Grand Duke Cosimo II around 1620, it was first installed in the rooms on the first floor which were expressly decorated by Pietro da Cortona and Ciro Ferri with a vast allegoric scheme which alluded to the glories of the Medici family. The Gallery was then added to uninterruptedly by the various grand dukes and princes of the house of Medici and of Lorraine. In 1799 many of its paintings and intarsia panels were abducted by Napoleon who took them to France from whence they returned (but only in part) in 1815. Ferdinand II of Lorraine continued the decoration of the other rooms, renovating them in neoclassic style, and doubled the Gallery which his successor Leopold II, opened to the public in 1833.

The fame of the Pitti collections is based on various

exceptional groups of paintings by important artists such as Raphael, Titian, Andrea del Sarto, Rubens, Perugino and various groups of minor personalities. Notable is the number of historical portraits, another characteristic of the Gallery, whose charm is due to the sumptuous yet familiar atmosphere engendered by one of the few extant examples of a 17th-century picture gallery.

The most important works include the large tondo which Filippo Lippi painted in 1450 for a wealthy Florentine merchant with a *Madonna and Child* in the foreground and the *Birth of the Madonna* in the background. In addition to his famous portraits of Agnolo and Maddalena Doni and the *Portrait of a Lady* known as *La Velata*, Raphael is represented by his world-famous *Madonna della Seggiola* or *Madonna of the Chair*, painted in the artist's maturity. The theme of the Madonna and Child was particularly dear to Raphael (his *Madonna del Granduca* is also in the Gallery). In the *Madonna della Seggiola* the composition is perfectly fitted into the circular shape of the panel, while the color accentuates the feeling of depth and space.

A Giorgione-like *Concert* is by Titian. A warm golden tone prevails in the simple composition of three figures around a harpsichord. The Gallery also owns five splendid portraits by the same artist, including the portrait of a man, also known as *The Man with Grey Eyes*.

Peter Paul Rubens, the greatest 17th-century Flemish painter, is represented in the Pitti by a dozen of his works. Notable is the enormous canvas of *The Consequences of War*, the composition of which is characterized by the fluid movement of the figure of Mars as he disentangles himself ·from Venus' embrace to follow Dischord who drags him away.

The scabrous realism and the intensity of feeling which characterize all the work of Michelangelo Merisi known as Caravaggio come to the fore in his *Sleeping Cupid* where «the serene image of a sleeping youth corresponds to the ideals of the painter, who uses light to reveal what the real subject is - the innocent sleep of a child» (M. Chiarini).

Among the numerous other important works bare mention must be made of Filippino Lippi's *Death of Lucrezia*; Andrea del Sarto's *Assumption of the Madonna*; the *Lament over the Dead Christ* by Fra' Bartolomeo; the *Portrait of Cardinal Bentivoglio* by Antonio Van Dyck; Perugino's *Madonna del Sacco*; a *Sacra Famiglia* by Guercino.

After 1919 precious objects of varying provenance (previously kept in the private apartments of the Palace) were put on display in the frescoed rooms on the ground floor of the left wing of Palazzo Pitti in what is now the **Museo degli Argenti**. These treasures which had been accumulated by the Medici family and the house of Lorraine constitute, despite dispersion, a collection that is of great importance both in its quantity and quality, and which includes precious stones, cameos, incised gems, figurines, porcelain, objects in amber, coral and ivory, gilded and embossed silver, etc. The original core dates back to Lorenzo the Magnificent, while the collection was further enriched as late as the 19th century, with the treasure of the Bishop of Salzburg, brought from Austria by Ferdinand III of Lorraine when he returned from temporary exile in 1814.

In the rooms of the top floor of Palazzo Pitti is the **Gallery of Modern Art**, founded around 1860, rearranged in 1910 and subsquently added to. It offers a complete picture of Tuscan 19th- and 20th-century painting and contains important examples of other Italian 19th-century schools, prominent among which are the schools of Piedmont and of Naples. A distinction is made between the academic nucleus and the group of Florentine Macchiaioli painters, including Giovanni Fattori, Silvestro Lega, Adriano Cecioni, Telemaco Signorini and others. The part dedicated to contemporary art, even though rich, is not nearly as important and is much more limited with respect to the Italian movements.

Under the instigation of Grand Duke Peter Leopold, all the schools of drawing which existed in Florence were reunited into a single Academy in 1784. The grand duke's intentions also included the establishment of a Gallery of ancient painting to be used by the students for study purposes. The result was the **Galleria dell'Accademia**, quartered in the rooms which had previously been part of the old Spedale of San Matteo as well as the ex-convent of San Niccolò. Numerous pieces from churches and convents that had been suppressed were added onto the original collection. After 1913 the most valuable works were transferred to the Uffizi while another part went to make up the Gallery of Modern Art.

In 1873 when Michelangelo's colossal statue of *David* was transferred from the Piazza della Signoria, the Gallery became more important. Early in the 20th century some of Michelangelo's most interesting sculptures were placed in the tribune built specifically for the *David*. These were the statue of *Saint Matthew*, the four *Prisons* and in 1939 the *Palestrina Pietà*.

Today, after the Uffizi, the Galleria dell'Accademia is the most sought after and frequented museum in Florence. The most outstanding pieces are of course Michelangelo's masterpieces, above all the *David*, «synthesis of the ideals of the Florentine Renaissance» (Tolnay). The famous work was executed by the artist between 1501 and 1504 utilizing a piece of marble roughly trimmed by Agostino di Duccio and then abandoned in the courtyard of the Opera del Duomo as unusable. The colossal statue (over four meters high) expresses Michelangelo's great creative gifts, capable of infusing strength under tension into the beautiful limbs of the young man, and the firm will of conquering the enemy in the expression of the face.

A conspicuous group of Italian «primitives» is included in the Gallery's collection. One of the panels outstanding for its iconographic originality and expression, from the Convent of Santissima Annunziata, represents *Mary Magdalen and Scenes from her Life* and is attributed to an anonymous master of the Byzantine school in the second half of the 13th century.

Mention must be made of the famous wedding scene painted on the front panel of a chest, in line with a popular medieval and Renaissance custom. The so-called «Adimari chest», datable around the middle of the 15th century, represents the happy occasion with refined elegance and the exact depiction of the costumes and the surroundings. The small panel with the *Madonna and Child* has recently been attributed to Botticelli. Because the figures are set against a marine background it is known as the *Madonna del Mare*. Indeed the delicate image of the Virgin, and the «thoughtful melancholy of the features» and the «lyrical development of the linear movement» are typical of

Botticelli.

Other important works in the Galleria are an *Annunciation and Saints* by Lorenzo Monaco, the *Apparition of the Virgin to St. Bernard* by Fra' Bartolommeo, a *Madonna and Child with Saints* by Cosimo Rosselli, a *Pietà* by Giovanni da Milano and numerous other paintings by minor Tuscan painters (especially Florentine) of the 13th-16th centuries which make the Gallery a sort of complement to the Uffizi.

After the Convent was suppressed in 1866, the new **Museo di San Marco** was opened to the public on October 15, 1869. It was also known as «dell'Angelico» for, what with frescoes and panel paintings, it contains almost a hundred works by Guido di Pietro Tosini, born near Vicchio, whose religious name was Fra' Giovanni da Fiesole, known as Beato Angelico (1387-1455). «The most fascinating monographic museum known today» reunites practically all the panel paintings by the artist extant in Florentine territory together with the fresco cycle which Angelico and the wide circle of his pupils (including Benozzo Gozzoli, Alessio Baldovinetti and Zanobi Strozzi) executed, beginning in 1438, on the walls of the cloister, of the dormitory and of the cells of the Convent of San Marco, renovated in those same years by Michelozzo. Among the most important works by the artist is without doubt the small panel of the *Flight to Egypt* which was once part, with 35 other scenes, of the decoration of the doors of the Silver Cabinet in Santissima Annunziata. «The body movements of the protagonists of the perilous voyage as they slowly advance is both subdued and sublime while a clear natural light illuminates and three-dimensionally defines figures and things» (R. Chiarelli).

The splendid panel of the *Deposition*, datable between 1435 and 1440, is considered the zenith of the artist's style in the skillful composition of the groups of figures, with Christ boldly set on a diagonal, in the use of the light which permeates the entire scene, in the «insuperable brilliance of the color». One of Angelico's other major works, dated between 1431 and 1440, is the panel painting of the *Virgin and Child with Saints Peter Martyr, Cosmas, Damian, John Evangelist, Lawrence and Francis*, originally in the ex-Convent of Annalena from which the panel takes its name. Here, too, the color, with its bright tones, is the principal virtue of the work which is also outstanding in being the first example of a «unified altarpiece», a painting in other words that does not present the traditional division into compartments. On the first floor the austere bareness of the Monastery with its huge dormitory covered by a trussed timber roof and the small cells is brightened by the frescoes Fra Angelico painted there between 1439 and 1445. The various scenes, most of which represent episodes from the life of Christ, include what may be the artist's masterpiece: the famous *Annunciation* which has been defined as one of the «most perfect and spiritual interpretations of this fascinating and poetic theme», which the friar-artist so dearly loved.

In 1859 the Provisory Government of Tuscany decreed the founding of a Historical Museum to be installed in the rooms of the old *Palazzo del Podestà* or *Bargello*, which at the time was still a prison. A few years later, in 1874, the Museum became primarily a museum of sculpture (transferred from the Uffizi which had been rearranged) and of the minor arts.

Since then it has continued to grow: in 1888 the fine Carrand collection of European art from the Middle Ages to the 16th century was left to the Museum; in 1899 it received the Ressman collection; and in 1906 the Franchetti collection of textiles. The Italian State which had replaced the Provisory Government saw to it that the most important works of Florentine sculpture, especially from the Renaissance, were added to the collections. The **Museo Nazionale** or **del Bargello** is therefore now the leading museum in Italy and one of the most important in the world thanks to its collections of the minor arts and of sculpture. The number and quality of works by Donatello, the Della Robbias and all the other great Renaissance sculptors make the museum one of a kind. The collection of 16th-century sculpture, including works by Michelangelo, Cellini and Giambologna, is also outstanding. It is impossible not to mention the arms section, the basis of which was the Armeria Medicea, nor the other sectors -goldwork and enamels, objects in iron, medieval ivories, Italian Renaissance majolica, textiles, seals, medals, Renaissance bronzes. The Museum owns various works by Michelangelo including the famous *Pitti Tondo* a work which «convinces in the superb beauty of the image», as well as the so-called *Bust of Brutus* (supposed to be the idealized portrait of Lorenzo de' Medici, who killed the hated Duke Alessandro) and his *Bacchus*, an early work, a marble bas-relief representing the *Martyrdom of Saint Andrew* and an unfinished statue of *David*, formerly called Apollo.

Since 1887 the grand hall of the *Salone del Consiglio Generale* has contained the collection of works by Donatello and other Florentine sculptors of the first half of the 15th century. The basic work in the affirmation of the early Renaissance style, Donatello's marble statue of *St. George*, dominates the hall from the center of the back wall. The figure was made in 1416 for the edicule of the Arte dei Corrazzai e degli Spadai in Orsanmichele. Vasari noted «the beauty of youth and the valor in arms, a vivacity that was proud and terrible, and a wonderful gesture of movement within that stone». Towards the center of the hall is Donatello's *David*, a bronze statue on a marble base made around 1430 for the Medici in the courtyard of whose palace it stood for the entire 15th century. The first Renaissance nude, of a harmonious and serene beauty, the sculpture is animated in the youth's head by «a subtle psychological vitality» apparently reflecting on the deed just done. The *St. John*, a marble statue with a «profoundly ascetic expression», the bronze statuette of *Athis* (Cupid) and other minor works are also by Donatello.

The other great masters of Renaissance sculpture are also represented with outstanding works: from the small bronze by Antonio del Pollaiolo of *Hercules and Antaeus* to the so-called *Lady with a Bunch of Flowers* by Verrocchio; from Giambologna's elegant *Mercury* to the colossal bronze bust of *Cosimo de' Medici* realized by Cellini between 1545 and 1547.

The Museo Nazionale also contains a representative group of works of the art of Luca Della Robbia, among the earliest and purest creations of the artist, one of the renovators of Renaissance art, whose fame is unjustly linked more to the invention of glazed terracotta.

Another Florentine museum full of works of art that refer especially to the late Renaissance and the Baroque is **Palazzo Vecchio**. Its interiors still preserve the splendor they had when the Palazzo was the residence of the Signoria and then the palatial residence of Cosimo I. The *Salone dei Cinquecento*, built as a container for the Consiglio Generale del Popolo, instituted with the reforms solicited by Savonarola, was restored and freshly decorated by Vasari, on commission from the house of Medici. The beautiful ceiling is divided into panels with allegories and histories of Florence while on the walls precious tapestries with episodes from the life of St. John the Baptist, woven by the Arazzeria Medicea, hang below large frescoes by Vasari. Different groups of statues by various artists complete the decoration of the Salone. The powerful dramatic expression of Michelangelo's *Victory*, represented as a young man who conquers brute force, stands out above the others.

Francesco I's *Studiolo* is a late Renaissance gem. Vincenzo Borghini suggested the themes which Vasari visualized on the walls of this precious and silent «receptacle». The paintings on the ceiling are by Francesco Morandini, known as Poppi.

The second floor contains the so-called *Hall of the Elements*, the name given to the whole suite of rooms. Built by Del Tasso around the middle of the 16th century and later modified by Vasari, the hall takes its name from the mythological allegories frescoed on the walls and ceiling. Vasari was flanked by various artists and decorators, in particular Cristofero Gherardi known as Doceno. The *Sala dei Gigli*, realized by Benedetto da Maiano, took its name from the golden fleur-de-lys decorations on the walls, which refer to the relationship that existed between the Florentine republic and the Kingdom of France. The frescoes on the walls are the work of Domenico Ghirlandaio and his assistants. They were executed between 1481 and 1485. In the apartment of Eleonora of Toledo, consort of Grand Duke Cosimo I, note should be taken of the *Green Room* with grotesques on the vaulting, the *Writing Room (Scrittoio)* with a ceiling by Francesco Salviati, as well as the fine *Chapel*, entirely painted by Bronzino, with a *Deposition* on the altar, with the figures of Mary and the Archangel Gabriel at the sides. Other rooms in the Palazzo which deserve at least a mention are the *Sala dei Dugento*, the *Quarters of Leo X*, the *Audience Hall*, the *Chapel of the Signoria*, the *Sala del duca Cosimo I*, the *Sala di Clemente VII*, etc.

The seat of the *Museo dell'Antica Casa Fiorentina* is **Palazzo Davanzati**, built in the 14th century by the noble Florentine family of the Davizzi which kept it until 1516 when it was sold to the apostolic protonotary Onofrio Bartolini. In 1523 it was once more sold to Bernardo Davanzati in whose family it remained until the 19th century. In 1951 the Palazzo was bought by the State and became a museum (early in the century the owner Elia Volpi had already seen to its restoration, furnishing the rooms with antiques). The interior decoration, which attempts to reproduce the characteristics of the patrician dwelling of the 14th century, is simple but refined and consists of furniture, decorative objects, paintings (all originals), historied chests, objects of daily use, which testify to a «poetically distant» life.

There are also many Museums in Florence unjustly classified as «minor», each of which would be the pride and joy of a city. From the *Museo dell'Opera del Duomo*, to the *Casa Buonarroti*; from the *Museo Horne*, to the *Bardini Museum*; from the *Museo di Santa Croce*, to the *Opificio delle Pietre Dure*, (workshop of semiprecious stones), to the *Museo Mediceo* in the *Palazzo Medici-Riccardi*. Not to mention the famous private Galleries such as the *Pinacoteche Corsini* and *Ferroni* and then the *Museo Archeologico*, the *Museo di Firenze com'era* and other Museums which contain specialized collections, such as the *Museo Stibbert*, which contains above all arms of all periods and countries, the *Museo degli Strumenti Musicali Antichi*, the *Museo dei Gessi*, the *Museo delle Porcellane*, etc.

We can only cite a few of the masterpieces which form part of the above-named collections. For example the **Museo dell'Opera del Duomo** which takes its name from the antique glorious magistrature which superintended the works on the Florentine Cathedral, the Opera del Duomo, contains a series of sculptures once kept in the Duomo, in the Baptistery or on Giotto's Campanile. These include some exemplary statues by Arnolfo and by Donatello and by Michelangelo, the stupendous marble panels by Andrea Pisano, the two wonderful choir stalls, which were executed respectively by Luca della Robbia and by Donatello for the tribune of the Duomo, as well as a wealth of other works by lesser artists which testify to the evolution of the tradition of Florentine sculpture from the Middle Ages to the Renaissance.

Casa Horne in the Via dei Benci formerly belonged to the Albertis and then to the Corsi family and represents a typical example of a Florentine patrician house of the 15th century. The collection housed there is the fruit of the passion and taste of Herbert P. Horne, an English scholar who acquired the Palazzo in the 19th century and lived there. In addition to a fantastic collection of drawings by Tiepolo, the original collection consisted of works by Giotto, Piero di Cosimo, Beccafumi and Vecchietta. Renaissance furniture, ceramics, miniatures, etc. complete the whole and give life to the rooms.

The **Museo di Casa Buonarroti** is housed in the building Michelangelo acquired in 1508 from Benedetto di Andrea Bonsi and which a nephew of the artist's later had decorated inside with a cycle of frescoes which exalted the glory of his ancestor. These paintings constitute a sort of anthology of Tuscan 17th-century painting for they were painted by the leading Tuscan artists of the period: Jacopo da Empoli, Giovanni da San Giovanni, Jacopo Vignali, Bilivert, etc. But Casa Buonarroti is above all a Michelangelo Museum for it contains a collection of drawings, sketches, models by the great artist as well as his early works: the *Madonna of the Stairs*, executed around 1490-1492, and the *Battle of the Centaurs*.

The **Museo dell'Opera di Santa Croce** is set up in what was once the Refectory of the greatest Franciscan convent in Florence. Frescoes by Taddeo Gaddi, including a **Last Supper**, decorate the back wall of the vast room. The Museum brings together painting from the 14th to the 16th centuries, as well as sculpture and architectural elements which formerly belonged to the church. Outstanding are the gilded bronze statue by Donatello of *St. Louis of Tolouse*, Cimabue's famous *Crucifix*, seriously damaged in the flood of 1966, a fresco by Domenico Veneziano with *St. John the Baptist and St. Francis*.

The **Bardini Museum** was left to the City of Florence by Stefano Bardini, an antique dealer, and contains collections of sculpture, in particular decorative, furniture, ceramics, paintings, tapestries and arms. Some of the pieces of major importance are a *Madonna and Child*, a bust in terracotta derived from Jacopo della

Quercia, an altarpiece by Andrea della Robbia, with the *Madonna and Angels*, a statue of *Charity* attributed to Tino da Camaino, a panel by Antonio del Pollaiolo, representing *St. Michael Archangel* and numerous other sculptures in terracotta or polychrome wood of the 14th-15th centuries.

The **Palazzo Medici-Riccardi**, built in the Via Larga by Michelozzo for Cosimo il Vecchio, houses the Museo Mediceo in some of the rooms on the ground floor. They contain portraits of the most important members of the family, a series of 16th-century tapestries, and documentary material as well as a *Madonna and Child* by Filippo Lippi. The famous *Journey of the Magi to Bethlehem*, a fresco by Benozzo Gozzoli, unfolds on the walls of the Chapel. It probably contains portraits of the figures who took part in the solemn horseback procession of the Greeks, who had come to Florence for the Council of 1439.

The **Corsini Gallery**, begun in 1765 by don Lorenzo Corsini, nephew of Clement XII is the most important private collection in Florence. It contains numerous 17th-century works and furnishes an ample picture of Italian and foreign painting of the time. The Gallery also owns a conspicuous group of paintings of the Florentine school of the 15th and 16th centuries. Among the most outstanding, mention must be made of Sustermans, of a *Madonna and Child with the Infant St. John*, by Pontormo, an *Annunciation* by Botticelli, a *Madonna and Child with Saints* by Luca Signorelli, and then paintings by Reni, Vanvitelli, Salvator Rosa, Volterrano and others.

The **Galleria Ferroni**, in which various paintings from the 15th-18th centuries are gathered together, was donated to the State by Marquis Ferroni in 1850 and installed in some of the rooms of the ex-Convent of Sant'Onofrio, formerly appertaining to the Franciscans of Foligno. The paintings, exhibited in the vestibule of the Convent and in the Refectory, include works by Filippino Lippi, Rosso Fiorentino, Lorenzo Monaco, Carlo Dolci, Salvator Rosa. On the back wall of the Refectory is the famous *Foligno Cenacolo* by Perugino and assistants, found fortuitously in 1845.

The **Museo delle Pietre Dure**, constituted by Pietro Leopoldo so as to bring together the famous intarsia works in semiprecious stone for which Florentine mosaics had been famous from the 15th century on, not only preserves many fine mosaics, mostly from the Uffizi, but is also concerned with the restoration and decoration of works in fine marble.

Begun by Grand Duke Leopold II in 1824 and then enlarged with gifts and purchases, the «Etruscan Collections» were the main core of the **Museo Archaeologico** of Florence, of fundamental importance for the study of Etruscan culture and art. The various sectors and collections are comprised of: the Etruscan-Greek-Roman Antiquarium, the Egyptian Museum (second in importance for Italy after Torino), the collection of Greek, Etruscan and Roman sculpture, the Collection of the Prehistoric Collection, Oriental and Greek, as a well as a Garden with reconstructed tombs and a collection of Pottery. Among the most important works mention should be made of the three large and famous Etruscan bronzes: the statue of *Minerva*, an imitation of a Greek work which recalls the style of Praxiteles, found in Arezzo in 1554; the *Chimera Wounded by Bellerophon*, also discovered in Arezzo in 1555 and restored by Cellini; the *Arringatore of the Trasimeno*, a monumental funerary statue of the 3rd century B.C.

representing Aulus Metellus addressing the people (it was found in 1566 in Sanguineto). The oustanding piece in the sector of «Vases and Terracottas» is the famous «François Vase», a deluxe crater, certainly a wedding gift, painted by the Greek artist Kleitias in the Athenian workshop of Ergotimos in the 6th century B.C. Noteworthy among the red-figure Attic vases are the two famous «Hydriae of Populonia», one with the myth of Venus and Phaon and the other with that of Venus and Adonis, and among the cups, those identified as being by «Chachrylion» by «Brygos» and «Douris». Mention should also be made of the polychrome sarcophagus of «Larthia Seianti, wife of Svenia», datable to between 217 and 147 B.C. found near Chiusi, as well as the other sarcophagus from Chiusi known as the sarcophagus «of the Obese Man», the statue in *pietra fetida* of the *Mater Matuta* seated on a throne with a child on her lap, with a marvelous severity of style, the Greek statue in bronze known as *Idolino* representing a young victor of the palestra who is pouring a libation on the altar of a god. Etruscan tombs and monuments have been reconstructed in the garden, mostly with authentic material brought there from their place of origin.

And lastly mention must be made of another minor Museum of great importance for the ancient topography of Florence, with its wealth of documents, drawings, architectural and decorative finds which testify to the character of the city in centuries past and above all give us an idea of what the quarters which were unthinkingly destroyed in modern times looked like. All this can be found in the **Topographical Museum of «Firenze com'era» (Florence as it was)** built around the documentation collected by G. Carocci during the demolition of the old center.

Florence also boasts a series of Scientific Museums. While they may not offer a complete picture of modern science, they do allow us to identify the moments that went into its making, in the ambit of which the city played a leading role.

The medieval *Palazzo dei Giudici* houses the glorious organism of the **Institute and Museum of the History of Science (Istituto e Museo di Storia della Scienza)** where scientific instruments and objects from the antique collections of the Medicis and from various donations are reunited. It was established in 1927, both for the purpose of organically and publicly exhibiting the historical-scientific masterpieces preserved in Florence, and for educational purposes, promoting all the studies and research that refer to the history of science. It is just what the name indicates - an Institute-Museum - and it has two rich specialized libraries, restoration laboratories, storerooms, a planetarium, rooms for lectures and audio-visual presentations, etc. Among the most famous relics are Galileo's instruments and those used for the experiments carried out in the Accademia del Cimento; the armillary sphere, or planetary system according to Ptolemy, built by Antonio Santucci between 1588 and 1593 for Ferdinand I; antique astrolabes; measuring instruments; galvanometers; batteries and various apparata that belonged to Alexander Volta; navigation instruments, etc.

The *Palazzo Nonfinito* houses another important Florentine scientific museum: the **Museo Nazionale di Antropologia ed Etnologia**, founded (the first of its kind in Italy) in 1869 by Paolo Mantegazza, and subsequently greatly enlarged. It contains fine collections and significant documentary evidence of the culture of most of the extra-European peoples, the result of expeditions effectuated in the last decades of the 19th century and in our century in various regions of Asia, Africa and the Americas.

Grand Duke Peter Leopold was responsible for the foundation, in 1775, of the *Imperiale Regio Museo di Fisica e Storia Naturale*, known as **La Specola** because the same grand duke also set up an astronomical and meteorological observatory. Subsequently redimensioned, the Museum, which is situated in the antique *Palazzo Torrigiani* in the Via dei Serragli, now limits itself to exhibiting the rich zoological collections it owns, including a precious entomological collection of over two million insects. Outstanding are the anatomical models in wax made in the old wax sculpture workshop of the Museum, which was active until the end of the 19th century. This collection is absolutely unique, the work in great part of Clemente Susini, and marvelous in the lifelikeness of the more than 600 models.

The foundation of the **Museo Botanico Fiorentino** dates back to 1842 when it was proposed to found a central Italian Herbarium on the occasion of the III Congress of Botany. Upon the Grand Duke's approval which was immediately forthcoming, rich collections of plants (Parlatore, Morris, Barbieri) found their way to the city. In 1845 the herbarium and manuscripts of Pier Antonio Micheli which Giovanni Targioni had obtained in 1738 and then enlarged, were acquired. Of the subsequent donations, the finest were those of Filippo Barker Webb and Beccari. Altogether the Museum now has a herbarium consisting of over 500,000 specimens.

The Museum is part of the Botanical Institute, which includes a school, with a laboratory and a library, and a *Botanical Garden*. Originally the Garden was the **Giardino dei Semplici (Herb Garden)**, founded by Cosimo I in 1545, who charged Tribolo with building a garden to be entrusted to the famous botanist Luca Ghini. After a period in which rather unqualified directors succeeded each other, the Garden was entrusted in the beginning of the 18th century to Pier Antonio Micheli, the famous botanist, who added many fine specimens. Later the arrangement and even the architecture of the old «Giardino dei Semplici» were considerably modified and the garden did not become what it is today until the early 19th century, under the direction of Ottaviano Targioni Tozzetti. Today except for a yew planted by Pier Antonio Micheli in 1720 the oldest trees date to the reorganization carried out by Targioni. Noteworthy, among others the collection of conifers and cycads.

The collections preserved in the **Museo fiorentino di Mineralogia e Litologia** were also begun by the first grand dukes of the Medici family, true pioneers in this field of science. In the 17th century Ferdinand II charged his personal doctor, the Dane Niels Stensen (Italianized into Niccolò Stenone), with the reordering of the collections. Stenone had a considerable number of samples brought into Florence from every part of the world and he set out to study them, contributing greatly to the birth of crystallography. Interest in the consistent collections continued under the house of Lorraine. In 1763 Targioni Tozzetti compiled an inventory of the «natural objects». Then in the 19th century the mineralogy collections, enriched by the fine Foresi collection (including minerals and rocks from the island of Elba), were transferred from the Imperial Regio Museo di Fisica e Storia Naturale (the Specola) to the present location in what were originally the stables of the grand dukes. The Museum is now articulated into five sectors: General Collection, Italian Collection, Collection of Cut Stones, Collection of Meteorites, Lithology Collection.

And lastly the richest Italian collections of paleontology and geology are housed in the **Museo di Geologia, Paleontologia e Geografia Fisica**, an annex of the Institute of the same name. The original nucleus of the collection was of course the collections of the Medici grand dukes, then enriched by the house of Lorraine and particularly, after the unification of Italy, by material from the Valdarno, which constitutes the principal part of the sector of Vertebrates. Of considerable interest is the human skull from Olmo, a subfossil important for our study of primitive man. The more recent *Museo Fiorentino di Preistoria* also depends on the Institute of Paleontology.

THE ART CENTERS

UFFIZI

An immense collection of paintings as well as sculpture and the decorative arts. Inside: the exhibition halls of the **Gallery**, the remains of the **Church of S. Piero Scheraggio**, the **Gabinetto dei Disegni e delle Stampe** and **Vasari's Corridor**, with its **collection of Self-portraits**.

GALLERIA DELL'ACCADEMIA (Via Ricasoli)

Contains a collection of works of sculpture including Michelangelo's *David*, the *Prisons*, the *Palestrina Pietà*, and the *St. Matthew*, Giambologna's *Rape of the Sabines*, as well as numerous paintings.

CHURCH AND MUSEUM OF SAN MARCO

Next to the church, the complex of the **Convent of S. Marco** with numerous works by Fra Angelico. Inside: the **Cloister**, the **Chapter Hall**, the **Refectory** and the **Hospice**. On the upper floor: the **cells**, including those of Savonarola and of Cosimo, and Michelozzo's **Library**.

PALAZZO PITTI

The largest palace in the city, with a spacious courtyard inside. It houses the **Royal Apartments**, the **Palatine Gallery**, the **Gallery of Modern Art** as well as the **Museo degli Argenti** and the **Coach Museum**.

BOBOLI GARDENS

Situated to one side behind the Palazzo Pitti. They contain **Buontalenti's Grotto**. Departing from the courtyard of the palace one encounters the **Amphitheater**, before continuing uphill to **Neptune's Fishpond**, near which the **Grand Duke's Casino** is situated; then down to the **Oceanus Fountain**.

GALLERIA PALATINA

Installed in the rooms on the first floor of Palazzo Pitti.
Collection begun by Cosimo II and organized with an eye to interior decoration inside sumptuously furnished rooms.

ARCHAEOLOGICAL MUSEUM (Via della Colonna)

Overlooking the **Garden** which contains reconstructions of antique architecture. At present being reorganized, it contains prestigious collections divided into sections: Egyptian, Etruscan, Greco-Roman, Eastern Mediterranean and the Collection of Ceramics.

ENVIRONS

FIESOLE

An Etruscan city with stretches of the ancient **city walls**. On the **Piazza Mino da Fiesole**: the **Cathedral of S. Romolo**, and the **Church of S. Maria Primerana**. In the Archaeological area: the **Museo Civico** with archaeological material from the **Theater**, the **Etrusco-Roman Temple**, and the **Baths**. Near the Belvedere, the **Basilica of S. Alessandro** and the **Franciscan Convent**.

UFFIZI

The gallery of the Uffizi is the most famous picture gallery in Italy and one of the best known in the world. It furnishes a complete panorama of the various schools of Florentine painting, represented by important works and authentic masterpieces. It also includes numerous collections of other Italian schools (particularly the Venetian) and a fine group of Flemish paintings, as well as the famous collections of self-portraits. To be noted also are the antique statues and an extensive collection of tapestries. The Uffizi was commissioned from Giorgio Vasari by the Medicis as administrative and judicial offices (thence the name). Begun in 1560 and finished twenty years later, the two wings with a loggiato at the bottom are connected by a third wing with arches along the Arno. On either side of the central courtyard powerful piers contain niches with 19th-century statues of illustrious Tuscans, while the upper floors of the building have windows (1st floor) and a running loggia (2nd floor).

*In addition to the **Gallery**, which is on the second floor, the building houses the **State Archives** which contain rare documents from the city's history. On the ground floor note should be taken of the remains of the Romanesque church of **San Piero Scheraggio** (brought to light and restored in 1971) with fine frescoes by Andrea del Castagno. On the first floor is the **Gabinetto dei Disegni e delle Stampe** (Drawing and Print Cabinet), an imposing*

Facing page, above: the side of the Uffizi overlooking the Arno.
Below: the courtyard of the Uffizi.

Above, left: Santa Trinita Madonna, by Cimabue; right: Ognissanti
Madonna, by Giotto. Below: the panel with Christ the Redeemer
and four Saints, by Meliore di Jacopo.

Above: the San Pancrazio Polyptych, by Bernardo Daddi. Left: The Annunciation, by Simone Martini.

Above, left: Madonna and Child with Angels, by Pietro Lorenzetti.
Right: Presentation in the Temple, by Ambrogio Lorenzetti.
Left: Crucifix with stories from the Pasion, by the Master of the
Bardi Saint Francis.

collection begun in the 17th century at the behest of
Cardinal Leopoldo de' Medici.
The visit to the Gallery begins on the second floor. This
great museum did not become public patrimony until
1737, a gift of Anna Maria Ludovica de' Medici, the last
of this prestigious family. The gallery consists of 45 rooms
divided into sections.

Above: Annunciation, by Leonardo da Vinci. Left: Adoration of the Shepherds, by Lorenzo di Credi.

158

Above: The Duke and Duchess of
Urbino, by Piero della Francesca.
Right: Madonna and Child with
Saints, by Ghirlandaio.

Above: Magnificat Madonna, by Botticelli. Facing page, above:
Primavera; below: Birth of Venus, both by Botticelli.

160

Above: the Portinari tryptyc by Hugo van der Goes. Left: The Adoration of the Magi by Gentile da Fabriano.

Above: Holy Family (Doni Tondo), by Michelangelo.

Above, left: Cosimo the Elder, by
Pontormo. Right: Madonna and Child, by
Giulio Romano. Left: Slaughter of the
Innocents, by Daniele da Volterra. Facing
page, above: Venus and Cupid, by
Alessandro Allori; below: Henriette of
France as Flora, by Jean Marc Nattier.

165

Above: detail of the head of Michelangelo's David. Facing page: Michelangelo's sculpture in the Tribune of the Accademia.

GALLERIA DELL'ACCADEMIA

The Gallery houses an extremely important collection of sculpture by Michelangelo. The room that leads to the tribune, hung with tapestries, contains the Palestrina Pietà, whose attribution to Michelangelo is controversial, the unfinished St. Matthew, made for the Florentine cathedral, and the four «Prisons» (or slaves) which were meant for the tomb of Julius II in St. Peter's in Rome, which was never finished, like these male figures who seem to be trying to free themselves from the marble grip.
At the center of the spacious **Tribune** *is the original of the David (1501-4) commissioned from the great sculptor to replace Donatello's Judith on the balustrade of the Palazzo dei Priori. The room also contains an important collection of paintings of the Tuscan school of the 13th and 14th centuries.*

Three **small rooms** *are to the right of the* **Tribune** *and contain various* **shrines** *attributed to Bernardo Daddi and a fine Pietà by Giovanni da Milano. To the left another series of three small rooms which contain works by famous masters of the 14th century: of note are a fine Polyptych by Andrea Orcagna, and two series of panels representing Scenes from the Life of Christ and Scenes from the Life of St. Francis, by Taddeo Gaddi. To the left of the Tribune there is another large hall containing works of the Florentine 15th century, including Lorenzo Monaco's Annunciation, Filippino Lippi's St. John the Baptist and the Magdalen, the Madonna of the Sea, attributed either to Botticelli or Filippino Lippi, and a fine panel from a wedding chest, known as the Adimari wedding chest, by an unknown Florentine painter of the 15th century.*

Facing page, above: three of Michelangelo's « Prisons »; below, left to right: a « Prison », St. Matthew, and the Palestrina Pietà. Above: the room in the Galleria dell'Accademia with the Rape of the Sabines by Giambologna. Right: the Assumption and Saints by Perugino.

Left: a 14th-century panel with the Madonna and Child. Right: Botticelli's Madonna of the Sea. Below: the panel on the front of the Adimari wedding chest.

Facing page, above: the Cloister of S. Marco; below: the Room of the Hospice with works by Fra Angelico.

CONVENT AND CHURCH OF SAN MARCO

The **Convent** already existed in the 12th century. In 1437 Cosimo the Elder commissioned Michelozzo with the restructuration and it therefore became the first Florentine convent structure to be built in elegant essential Renaissance form. The lovely **Cloister** has simple elements in stone with brick cornices; on the ground floor the space is enclosed by airy arcades. On the first floor there are fine lunettes frescoed by Poccetti, Rosselli, Coccapani, Vanni, Cerrini, Dandini and other illustrious artists. The main entrance to the convent lies to the right of the **Church of San Marco**. This too was restored in 1437 by Michelozzo. It was later renovated by Giambologna (1580) and then by Silvani (1678). The simple facade was redone between 1777 and 1780 by Gioacchino Pronti. The linear interior has an outstanding carved and gilded ceiling. Of interest is the **Sacristy**, which contains the sarcophagus with the bronze statue of St. Antoninus (1608), and the adjacent **Chapel of St. Antoninus**, decorated by Giambologna, Francavilla, Alessandro

Facing page: the Refectory of S. Marco with the fresco of the
Crucifixion and of Providence by Sogliani. Above: Crucifixion by
Fra Angelico; below: Last Judgement, also by Fra Angelico.

Above: Girolamo Savonarola's antecell and, left, one of the cells frescoed by Fra Angelico; facing page, above: Fra Angelico's Deposition, and, below: Ghirlandaio's Last Supper in the Small Refectory of S. Marco, a variation of the one in Ognissanti.

Allori; the frescoes in the dome are by Poccetti. But the true center of attraction of this religious complex is without doubt the Convent. It is well known that an exceptional artist, Fra Angelico, lived and worked within these ancient walls. Most of the frescoes in the **Cloister** *(particularly beautiful are the* Crucifix with St. Dominic *at the entrance and the lunette over the door with* St. Peter Martyr*) are his. He also painted the* St. Dominic *in the* **Chapter Hall** *and a splendid* Crucifixion *inside; a* Pietà *over the door of the* **Refectory***; Jesus as a Pilgrim over the* **Hospice** *door, and inside, the* Madonna dell'Arte dei Linaioli, *the* Last Judgement, *the* Stories of Jesus, *the* Deposition. *Through the* **Refectory**, *with a large fresco by G. A. Sogliani (1536) of the* Crucifixion *and* Providence, *stairs lead to the upper floor, where Fra Angelico's* Annunciation *is most striking. The corridor leads to Michelozzo's* **Library** *and, at the end of the corridor, to* **Cosimo's Cell** *with a* Crucifix *by Angelico in the antecell and the* Adoration of the Magi *in the cell. In the corridor to the left is the* Madonna Enthroned with Saints, *and then other splendid works by Fra Angelico are to be found in the cells which open off the corridor; the* Annunciation, *the* Transfiguration, Jesus before the Praetor, *the* Maries at the Sepulcher, *the* Coronation, *the* Presentation in the Temple. *At the end of the corridor is* **Savonarola's Cell** *(the* Portrait *of the martyr is by Fra Bartolomeo). A staircase to the right leads into the* **Small Refectory** *with a large fresco of the* Last Supper *by Domenico Ghirlandaio (a version of the more famous one in Ognissanti).*

PALAZZO PITTI

The most imposing of the Florentine palaces dates to 1457 and was probably designed by Brunelleschi. Ammannati enlarged it in the 16th century. The facade (205 m. long and 36 m. high) is covered by a powerful rustication in enormous blocks of stone. The only decorative element are the crowned lion heads set between the window corbels on the ground floor. The two projecting wings date to the period of the Lorrainers. The large arched portal leads through an atrium into Ammannati's **courtyard** which lies lower than the hill of Boboli which with its gardens forms the back of the building. The **Royal apartments** and the **Palatine Gallery** are on the first floor; on the second is the **Gallery of Modern Art**. The palace also contains the **Museo degli Argenti** and the **Museo delle Carrozze**.

BOBOLI GARDENS

These gardens comprise the largest monumental green area in Florence. Their history goes back over four centuries, for Cosimo I commissioned the designs from Niccolo Pericoli, known as Tribolo, in 1549. Work was continued by Ammannati, Buontalenti and Parigi the Younger. Noteworthy places are: **Buontalenti's Grotto** (1583); the **Amphitheater** with the Roman basin and the Egyptian obelisk at the center; **Neptune's Fishpond**; the statue of Plenty by Giambologna and Tacca (1563); the **Grand Duke's Casino**, the **Cavalier's Garden**; Parigi's **Fountain of the Ocean**.

This page: Palazzo Pitti and the piazza. Facing page, above: the Bacchus Fountain and Neptune's Fishpond in the Boboli Gardens; below: the back of Palazzo Pitti.

Facing page, above: the Room of Saturn and, below, the Room of the Niches in Palazzo Pitti. Above: Raphael's Madonna of the Chair in the Palatine Gallery.

PALATINE GALLERY

The Palatine Gallery, which is the second museum for extension and importance after the Uffizi, contains works of enormous value for the history of art. It was realized by Ferdinando II de' Medici with decoration by Pietro da Cortona. The works are placed according to a sixteenth century conception; the pictures are in fact displayed on the walls in an essentially decorative way. The collection was enriched by Cardinal Lorenzo de' Medici, by the last members of the Medici family, and by the Lorrainers. The Gallery is formed of many rooms dedicated to gods and mythological characters depicted in the decorations.

Above, left: Raphael's Madonna del Granduca; right: Madonna and four Saints by Andrea del Sarto. Left: Raphael's Madonna dell'Impannata (of the Linen Window).

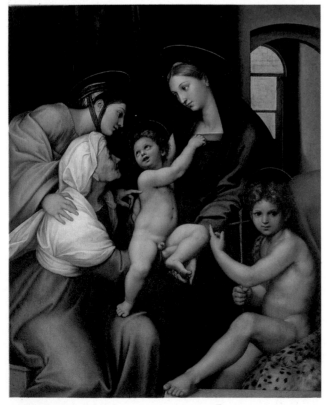

Raphael's Donna Velata.

Facing page, above, left: La Gravida, and, right, the Portrait of Maddalena Doni, both by Raphael; below: Madonna and Child by Filippo Lippi.

Right: Four Philosophers, and, below, the Consequences of War, both by Rubens.

Above, left: Vision of Ezekiel by Raphael; right: Assumption with Apostles and Saints by Andrea del Sarto. Left: Holy Family by Andrea del Sarto. Facing page: the two pictures with the Stories of Joseph hebrew by Andrea del Sarto.

ARCHAEOLOGICAL MUSEUM

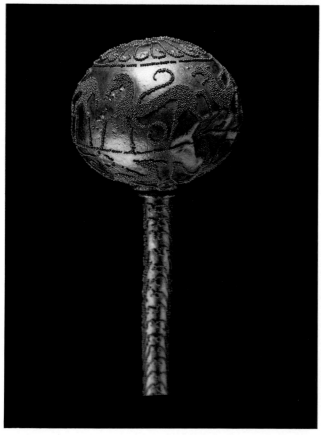

Its rich collections of Egyptian, Etruscan, Greek and Roman art make this museum, which is installed in the 17th-century **Palazzo della Crocetta**, one of Italy's most outstanding. The museum originated with the private collections of the Medicis and of the Grand Dukes. Of particular note in the Egyptian department, which was first instituted in 1824, are the sculpture of the Goddess Hathor nursing the Pharaoh, the polychrome relief of the Goddess Hathor with the Pharaoh Sethos I, and the bas-relief of the Goddess of Truth Maat. Outstanding in the collections of vases and terra cottas in the Graeco-Roman Antiquarium is the famous François Vase, a Greek work of the 6th century B.C., found in an Etruscan tomb. The crater, which was probably a wedding gift, was painted by Kleitias and comes from the workshop of the Athenian potter Ergotimos. It was named after Alessandro François who discovered it in Fonte Rutella (Chiusi) in 1845. The vase is decorated with heroic-mythological scenes in black-figure painting. Mention in the Graeco-Roman section must be made of the bronze statue known as Idolino (Attic-Peloponnesian school of the 5th cent. B.C.). The collection of Etruscan art, which includes material from more than three hundred years of study, is particularly fine. The collection abounds in sarcophagi, cinerary urns, bronzes, weapons, and objects of daily use. Particularly striking in the field of sculpture are the statue of the Arringatore, representing the orator Aulus Metellus, found near the Trasimene Lake (funerary art of the 3rd century B. C.), and the Chimaera wounded by Bellerophonte discovered in Arezzo in 1555, a 5th-century B.C. bronze with the body of a lion and the head of a goat on its back (the tail in the form of a snake is not original).

Facing page, above: the Chimaera of Arezzo; below: an Etruscan pin in gold from Vetulonia. This page, above: the François Vase from Chiusi; below: a gold bracelet from Vetulonia.

Facing page, above: view of the two knolls of Fiesole; below: Piazza Mino da Fiesole. This page, above: the Church of S. Francesco, and, right, the Roman Theater.

FIESOLE

*This ancient Etruscan city, standing on its hill, dominates Florence. The center consists of the beautiful **Piazza Mino da Fiesole** where the **Cathedral of S. Romolo** is situated. The Church, founded in the 11th century, contains the Salutati Chapel, with frescoes of the 15th century by Cosimo Rosselli and the tomb of Bishop Salutati, by Mino da Fiesole. The **Bishop's Palace** (11th cent.) and the old **Church of S. Maria Primerana** lie across from the Cathedral. Not far off is the **Church** and the **Convent of S. Francesco** (14th cent.), which houses the **Ethnographic Museum of Missions** with important Etruscan finds. The **Archaeological Civic Museum** and the wonderful **Roman Theater**, dated to the 1st century B.C., can be rapidly reached from the square. Nowadays the theater is usually used for numerous theatrical and cinematographical events. Nearby are the **Roman Baths** and the **Etrusco-Roman Temple**. The **Bandini Museum** with its sculptures and paintings from the 13th to the 15th century and the old **Basilica S. Alessandro** must not be overlooked.*

189

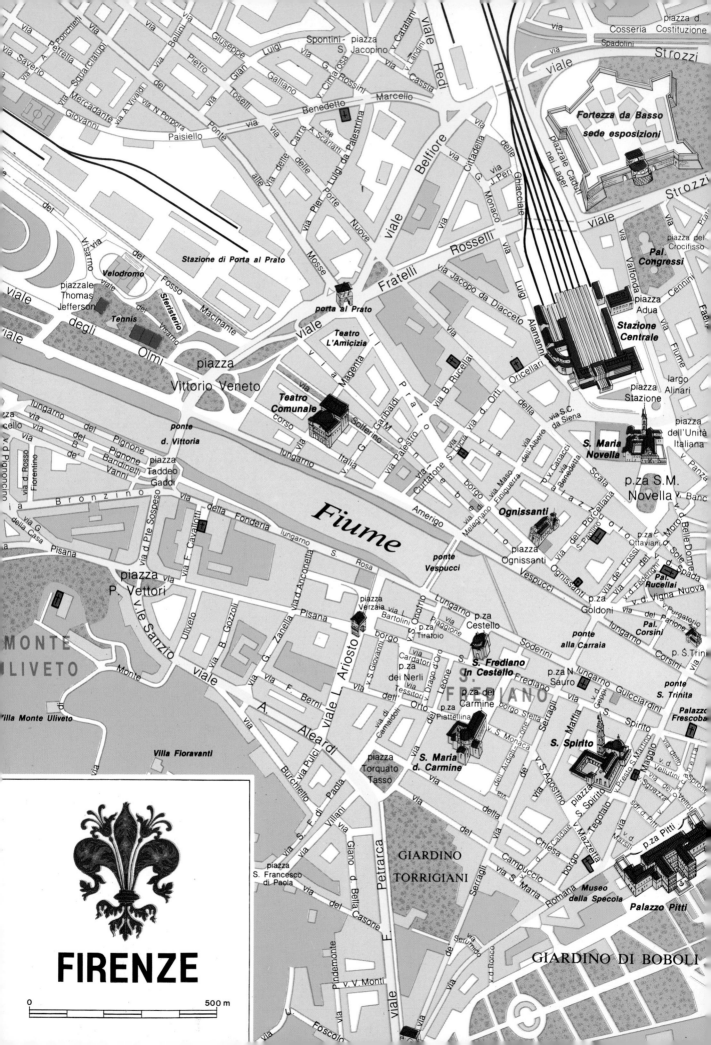

INDEX